Introduction: The Rainbow

'God said, this is the sign of the covenant which I now make between myself and you and every living creature with you for all ages to come: I now set my bow in the clouds and it will be the sign of the covenant between me and the earth. When I gather the clouds over the earth and the bow appears in the clouds, I shall recall the covenant between myself and you and every living creature . . .'

Our title has been chosen because its symbolism has much to say that is not only full of hope but also consoling and encouraging for us in the teaching profession.

The rainbow is a biblical symbol which speaks to us of hope. It appears in the sky at the point where the sun shines through the clouds and rain. As you face the daily challenges of life in your school community there are many moments when one wonders if the clouds and rain will ever cease! It is good to have a gentle reminder at the centre of the curriculum that all will be well.

The rainbow appears in scripture as a symbol which reminds us of God's promise after the flood that he will never again destroy the whole world. The rainbow is a sign for humanity that our God is with us in the daily struggle to build a just and peaceful society where all men and women can live in peace, enjoying their fair share of the world's resources. This was the first covenant and promise made between God and humanity. Unlike the later covenant with Moses on Mount Sinai, it was not just a covenant with the chosen people of Israel but with the whole human race.

The rainbow is also a reminder to us that in our schools and wider communities there are people who have not experienced being part of this covenant between God and humanity. Yet just as God recognized what could be between himself and humankind, so we too remember that the promise made by God is for those of other faiths and of none.

The rainbow is a symbol which reminds us that our God is a loving and faithful God who will not test us beyond our limits, just as Yahweh did not allow Abraham to pass through the passage way between the slaughtered animal halves (Genesis 15:1-18) but entered into a promise that recognized our frailty and weakness. He alone made the Covenant — promising that in spite of our unfaithfulness, he would never desert us. This is something totally unique, a contract between partners where the stronger allows the other to enjoy all the security of the partnership while at the same time recognizing that they may not be able to maintain their part of the agreement.

The liturgical year too is full of colour . . . colours of the rainbow.

1

Why we believe that God has a relationship with all human beings of all faiths

• Before there were any Israelites, Noah understood that God promised the human race that the rainbow would be the sign of the covenant between God and the whole human race; God would never again destroy every living creature in a flood.

'As long as earth endures, seed-time and harvest, cold and heat, summer and winter, day and night will never cease.' Genesis 8:22

• Later God called Abraham to found a special people — the people of Israel. As time went on, other peoples split off from the Israelites. Abraham's son Ishmael became the father of the Arab peoples. The Canaanites were descended from Ham, one of Noah's sons.

'Isaac is the one through whom your name will be carried on. But the slave-girl's son [Ishmael] I shall also make into a great nation.' Genesis 21:12-13

• So the Israelites thought of themselves as the chosen people of Yahweh. But they also knew that Yahweh wanted other peoples to exist, and wanted them to have their own lands.

'These were Japheth's sons, each in their respective countries, each with its own language, by clan and nation.' Genesis 10:5

• The Samaritans also worshipped Yahweh, but they thought Mount Gerizim was the best place to worship, rather than Mount Zion in Jerusalem. But they were also God's people.

Jesus said to the Samaritan woman at the well: "The hour is coming when you will worship the Father neither on this mountain nor in Jerusalem . . ." John 4:21

• God created all the peoples of the world and they all have a place. Now the world has become a global village, people of all cultures and religions can be found in the same place. But they are all God's people and they are all part of the human race with whom God made a covenant under the sign of the rainbow.

'When the bow is in the clouds I shall see it and call to mind the eternal covenant between God and every living creature on earth.' Genesis 9:16

The Promise of the
RAINBOW

A whole-school approach to P------------- Schools
for headteachers, clergy, ------------------ators

JUDITH ------- ------ SMN

*'I now set my bow in the clouds and it will be the
sign of the covenant between me and the earth.
When I gather the clouds over the earth and the
bow appears in the clouds, I shall recall the
covenant between myself and you and every
living creature.' (Genesis 9:13,16)*

GEOFFREY
CHAPMAN

Geoffrey Chapman
An imprint of Cassell Publishers Limited
Villiers House, 41/47 Strand, London WC2N 5JE, England

First published 1992

British Library Cataloguing-in-Publication Data
A catalogue record for this book is available from the
British Library.

ISBN 0-225-66655-3

Printed and bound in Great Britain by Short Run Press
Limited, Exeter

Contents

43023.

Foreword

The whole world of education seems to be in ferment. Not least is this true of religious education. The Catholic Bishops' Conference of England and Wales has responded in a number of ways. It has authorized the publication of a number of books outlining a national approach to the teaching of religion in our Catholic schools. At the same time a Roman Commission is about to publish a Catechism for the Universal Church. It is hoped that Bishops' Conferences and dioceses throughout the world will draw upon this catechism in the compilation of national and local catechisms and syllabuses. It is with these developments in mind that Sister Judith in her latest, remarkable book introduces a process of religious formation and growth which is quite breathtaking — and visionary. It involves families, parishes and schools and covers every aspect of a child's religious development. It should be of immense help to every religious educator. Her overview of Catholic religious education will enable headteachers and teachers to relate its principal themes to relevant areas of the National Curriculum. Her presentation will encourage teachers to integrate learning about the faith with celebrating that faith and living it. The book is based on her own vast experience as a teacher and as a religious adviser in the Diocese of Westminster. Throughout, she has consulted parents and teachers and tested her material in many schools. The result is a seminal work which will provide practical help and inspiration for generations to come.

✠ James O'Brien
 Bishop in Hertfordshire

Acknowledgements

The author would like to thank the following for their assistance in this project:

The Rt Rev James O'Brien, Bishop in Hertfordshire
Kathleen O'Gorman, Director of Education, Westminster Diocese
Westminster Diocese advisers
Rev Terry Burke MHM, theological consultant
Jack Kitching, HMI (retired)
Deirdre Madeley for the songs
CAFOD
Doreen Rolfe of Education Aid Africa
Holy Rood Infant and Junior Schools, Watford
Our Lady's Primary School, Hitchin
Sacred Heart Primary School, Ware
St Alban and St Stephen's Infant and Junior Schools, St Albans
St Albert the Great Primary School, Hemel Hempstead
St Bernadette's Primary School, London Colney
St Cuthbert Mayne Junior School, Hemel Hempstead
St Dominic's Primary School, Harpenden
St Joseph's Primary School, Bishop's Stortford
St Rose's Infant School, Hemel Hempstead
St Teresa's Primary School, Borehamwood
St Thomas of Canterbury Primary School, Puckeridge
St Vincent de Paul Primary School, Stevenage
Sr Joseph Marie Kasel, School Superintendent, Diocese of Colorado, USA
Paul Forte, Superintendent of Planning Development and the York
    Region RC Separate School Board, Diocese of Ontario, Canada
The York Region Elementary School Principals who assisted in the
    consultation process
Mrs MaryJo Rourke

Primary Resources: National Project
Much of the thinking behind *The Promise of the Rainbow* headteachers'
book and the teaching materials which will follow it, *The Rainbow People*,
has been greatly influenced by the developments within the National
Project of the Bishops' Conference of England and Wales. And we see
that the current primary resources that are on offer could quite easily fit
within the framework of this syllabus. What we are offering you is a
developmental structure for the whole school which will keep a clear
record of what each child has learnt, experienced and understood. It is a
clearly defined syllabus of Catholic teaching.

Recognizing God's presence
in all people

As we look back through salvation history, we see a fascinating development in the concept of a 'chosen people', a 'holy race', a 'people set apart'. Israel saw itself as *the people*, the first in the eyes of God. This is a tradition that has led to many a misunderstanding, often with devastating consequences, between the Jewish people and other nations. So too with Christianity and how it saw its place amongst world religions.

In its document, *The Religious Dimension of Education in a Catholic School (Gravissimum Educationis)*, the Church reminds us of our obligation to respect religious freedom:

> Not all students in Catholic schools are members of the Catholic Church; not all are Christians. There are, in fact, countries in which the vast majority of the students are not Catholics — a reality which the Council called attention to. The religious freedom and the personal conscience of individual students and their families must be respected, and this freedom is explicitly recognized by the Church.
>
> On the other hand, a Catholic school cannot relinquish its own freedom to proclaim the Gospel and to offer a formation based on the values to be found in a Christian education; this is its right and duty. To proclaim or to offer is not to impose, however; the latter suggests a moral violence which is strictly forbidden, both by the Gospel and by Church law.

Cultural diversity

In the report of the Working Party on Evaluating the Distinctive Nature of a Catholic School for the Bishops' Conference of England and Wales, Bishop Daniel Mullins of Menevia wrote:

> Each member of the school community should take seriously the variety of ways and stages along which God accompanies individuals so that they may discover truths about God. Cultural background and faith differences within the wider community, but especially if found within the school, provide a rich source of learning material for this at every level, psychological, social, emotional and intuitive, and therefore should be highly prized.

Part 1

PRINCIPLES - AND HOW TO PUT THEM INTO PRACTICE

A new vision:
foundation principles for RE

Catholics believe that Religious Education is not one subject among many
but the foundation of the entire educational process. The beliefs and values
it communicates should inspire and unify every aspect of school life. It
should provide the context for, and substantially shape, the school
curriculum, and offer living experience of the life of faith in its practical
expression.

(Bishops of England and Wales, 1988)

'Religious Education . . . should inspire and unify every aspect of school life'

Scripture and the tradition of Catholic teaching tell us that children have
an important place in the Christian Catholic community, and are unique
people in the eyes of God and the Church. This book is about ways to
help the whole school community bring this to life within a holistic
framework.

Religious Education should permeate the whole curriculum. It is not
something which can be 'bolted on' or 'slotted in' at a set time during the
day. What this framework provides is a way of approaching life in a
Catholic school community so that every aspect of the child's experience
is consistent with the aims of a Catholic education.

'. . . provide the context for, and substantially shape, the school curriculum'

Our aim is to place at the heart of the curriculum the essential truths of
our faith, and along with these the understanding of their significance in
terms of celebrating and living the Christian life. At every point, the
human being's response to God's gift of life and love must be
acknowledged. That will be the starting point and should be at every
level from reception up. For example, what should a child of five be
introduced to? How will these truths be approached and taught to
coincide with the psychological and spiritual development of the child?

Cross-curricular linking

No child can learn in a vacuum. It is essential that what is taught in RE
be linked closely into other key areas in the child's learning.

Understanding education as religious education

A Catholic school exists as a religious community. It is accepted that not all members will be at the same stage in their faith or in their understanding and practice. What we aim to offer is a way of helping our children to claim their identity as Christians in the Catholic tradition, to know *who* they are and *what* it means to be part of this community, to discover what it is to be a Christian at the turn of the century in our society. Who we are as Christians needs to be clearly presented to our children. This touches every aspect of our lives.

We need to understand and have confidence in our identity as Christians at this time in history and free ourselves to recognize the identity of people of other faiths in relation to God.

We are first and foremost *Christian*. That affects every aspect of our lives. Our choices as well as our lifestyle are all part of this.

What we are doing is this.

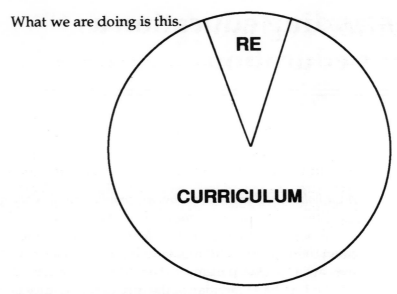

What we should be doing is this.

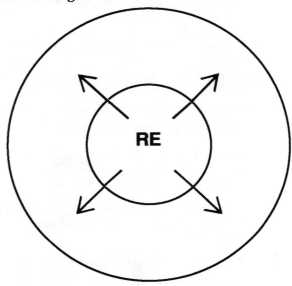

Which then does this.

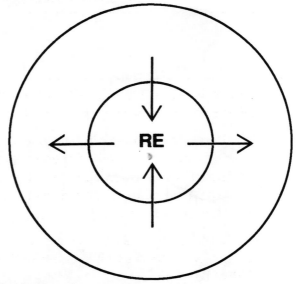

It's a **two-way process**.

The Catholic school

The Catholic school is called into being as a community of faith. It offers to children the experience of participation in this community which is conscious that its every act derives from God who is Father, Son and Spirit.

It seeks always to manifest its fidelity to God in every endeavour; each facet of its life is important and reflects God's purpose.

> In a world which ignores the human thirst for God, we are called to share the living waters of our faith.
>
> In a time when there is little reverence for the image of God in the human person, we are summoned to care for human life with an ultimate respect.
>
> In a culture where communication is increasingly commercialized, we are invited to prayer and worship.
>
> In a world marked by poverty, oppression and war, we are commanded to work for justice and peace.
>
> In a society marked by personality cults, we are called to bear witness to Jesus Christ, our Saviour and Lord, and to reverence him in the poor, the lowly, and the marginalized.
>
> In a time which often seems to be without goals or ennobling aspirations, we are challenged to declare ours and to dedicate our lives to their achievement.
>
> In an age which seems more fearful of the future, we are directed to give an account of the hope that is within us (1 Peter 3:15).
>
> (*This Moment of Promise*, Ontario Conference of Catholic Bishops)

Aim

The aim is to assist the Catholic school in its task of helping children to know God and experience the Christian life of his community.

The child's development in faith in a loving God begins at birth with the love and care of the family. Catholic parents bring their children to baptism to initiate them into the wider community of faith. From this begins a partnership of education in faith between the home, parish and then later the school.

The Catholic school seeks to support and develop the primary task of parents, who 'are the first teachers of their child in the ways of faith' (Rite of Baptism).

The pathway to learning here is the calendar of the Christian community, the Church's year, through celebrating its seasons in whole-school events.

The process embraces the total curriculum and life of the school. It invites priests, teachers, governors and parents to come together and celebrate the experience of children as they move through each stage of their Catholic education.

It takes seriously the whole person and looks for a balance between knowledge of doctrine (teaching), response to God (worship) and the personal and social development of the child (values).

It adopts a whole world approach which takes seriously the world issues of justice and peace facing us today, and the multi-cultural nature of our society and our faith. Throughout the process authentic ritual is encouraged and developed as an expression of a living response to the Gospel.

The headteacher, with the help of the RE co-ordinator

As one who exercises faithful leadership, the headteacher has to look to the following:

(a) promoting the school as a community of faith
(b) ensuring that the curriculum as a whole reflects Christian truth
(c) safeguarding and developing through his or her direction the whole work of witnessing to Jesus Christ
(d) assisting staff to pray and reflect together
(e) ensuring that every child is incorporated into the life of the school as a eucharistic community and is able to develop a clear understanding of what this means during his or her progress throughout the Catholic primary school
(f) promoting the full adoption of 'whole-school' liturgical celebrations which mark the significant moments of a child's year in the Christian community
(g) inspiring others to take forward the principles of formation set out below so that the whole curriculum is designed and shaped through fidelity to God's truth, order and beauty
(h) encouraging the consistent monitoring and assessment of each child's progress.

How can the headteacher carry out the responsibilities outlined above?

The head has quite specific and important tasks which are uniquely those of the leader of a Catholic school community. Some of the most vital are listed above, and this book assists headteachers in carrying out these tasks in the following ways:

• it suggests ways in which the staff may be helped to pray and reflect together, and how that might be seen to be important (see pages 13-16).

• it suggests ways in which every child can be incorporated into the life of the school as a eucharistic community, and grow in understanding of what this means. Careful study of the entire section on celebrating the eucharist in school (pages 20-42) should make the overall pattern clear; an acceptance of the urgent need for children's participation at an appropriate level will facilitate the staff's thinking and planning.

• it helps the headteacher to guide and facilitate the whole-school celebrations which make up the year of the Christian community. The Welcome celebration and the Sending Forth gathering, for example, enable children to know the reality of their baptismal invitation to be active members of God's family: the Catholic community of school and parish has a most serious obligation to assure each child of her or his place and worth and particular role in the community at every stage of growth (see pages 43-71).

• it sets Religious Education at the core of the curriculum and enables all to be certain of sound curriculum planning from the outset, so that the whole curriculum is designed and shaped through fidelity to God's truth, order and beauty (see pages 73-95).

• it provides a syllabus, flowcharts and a checklist to enable headteachers and teachers to ensure that their religious education syllabus is giving adequate and balanced attention to the liturgical year, the sacraments and the Church's teaching.

• it offers ideas for the consistent monitoring and assessment of each child's progress (see pages 96-97).

• it lays the foundation for educating young people in the social teaching of the Church, to enable them to grow into an awareness of the justice and peace issues of our time. Respect for life at all levels, whether it be plant, animal or human life, will be dealt with extensively over all the years of primary school.

The school chaplain

The involvement of the parish priest/school chaplain cannot be stressed too highly. You will notice throughout the syllabus that there are continual references to working with the parish and parents. Therefore, it is essential that your school chaplain is present and plays a key part in curriculum development discussions, so that the whole-school celebrations do not take place in a vacuum. They reinforce and develop the child's place in the faith community.

The chaplain has a very definite and important role to play and it is vital that the children and their parents see the school as part of a much wider community, that of the parish. It has been our experience in piloting this syllabus that the very best results for the children and the best experiences for the school came from preparation and planning sessions that involved the chaplain as well. Many school chaplains are only too willing to enter into the full life of the school if invited to do so.

It is a great help to them to know exactly what is expected of them and how they can contribute.

In one of our schools the parish priest took on the role of the school's story-teller. A special area was created by the top juniors, the governors invested in Bible story books for all age groups, some easy chairs, albeit second-hand, and a fruit juice and biscuit cupboard — the most popular feature of the area. The chaplain came regularly to his story area and the children would come individually, or in small groups, to have a story read, or for him to tell a story. For the pre-school children, in nursery and playschool, these regular visits to listen to Father tell stories proved to have a significant effect on how the children viewed the role of the priest in their life. From this experience the children now viewed the chaplain as an important friend whom they looked forward to seeing. The 'story-teller' is after all the first role of the priest — to proclaim the word.

Helping the school staff to reflect and pray together

With little or no non-contact time in a primary school it is extremely difficult for a school staff to find time to pray together. Yet this is one of the most profitable and enriching times that a staff can ever experience.

Teaching staff are hard pressed for time *all the time*, yet to find just a few quiet moments for them at the start of the day, or, if more appropriate, at the end of the day, not only calms everyone down, but allows for reflection and a deep level of sharing between the staff. Teachers desperately need to be allowed to have this opportunity. They need to relax, share their worries, concerns and struggles as well as the joys and successes and see the Lord working in their lives and in the lives of the children.

Support staff can also be encouraged to join in these prayer times. Caretakers are key figures in any school and have a significant effect on everyone's life. They too need this opportunity.

By bringing everyone together in this way, you are reinforcing the concept of being a faith community: one family, each person with individual responsibilities, but all working for the same end.

What to do

Many ways are available to help your staff to pray and reflect together. It is important to recognize that individuals will be at different points in their faith journey. Some will be quite comfortable praying with others, whilst for others it will be quite the opposite. This must not prevent the community from actually beginning to spend time in reflection and prayer together.

Begin very simply. Here are some examples.

Prayer board

At staff briefing on a Monday morning explain to the staff that it matters what is happening in each person's life, but often we are all so busy rushing around that we seldom have time to sit down and listen to one another. So, if the staff would like to pray together for an individual's special intention that week, a note can be put on the prayer board. Such notes can be signed or anonymous.

Scripture verse

Each week, or if you wish each morning, the staff can choose a verse of scripture to keep before them for the day. Someone might be invited to just say a few words about what it meant for them.

Special intentions from parents/children

These could be put on a board and/or shared each week with the staff and a few moments of silent prayer could follow for that intention.

At the end of the week

It is very important in a Christian community that the week does not end without a moment shared together in thanksgiving for all that has been accomplished and the opportunity taken for reconciliation and forgiveness.

In one of our primary schools in Hertfordshire I was deeply moved by one such experience.

The headteacher had been nothing less than a bear with a sore head for most of the week. What the staff did not know was that he had had a serious family problem blow up at the weekend. By Friday there was hardly a member of staff who had not been barked at and the children were giving him a very wide berth. Everyone had a bad week. The last thing they wanted to do was pray together. A staff meeting had been scheduled for 4p.m. We all sat there waiting for the inevitable crash as the head pounded through the door to begin the unwelcome meeting.

4.15p.m. and no headteacher. No one was going to go and look for him either!

The deputy (and aren't they always the ones who get these jobs?) made his way to the staff-room door to enquire as to the whereabouts of the headteacher. Just then the door opened and in walked a small girl holding the head's hand.

To everyone's amazement she led him to where there was an empty chair and as the head sat down climbed on to the chair beside him. Nothing like this had ever happened before. Total silence followed. Very quietly the head began to apologize for being late but explained to the staff that Amy had been talking to him very seriously. Her mother was going to be late and she had come to wait in his room as was the custom in that school. But she had been afraid to come in. Then the head turned to Amy and asked her to say why she was afraid to go into his office. In a way that only a five-year-old can do, she looked straight at

15

him and said,'Because you've been an old grouch.'

For a second there was a stunned silence! Then the staff room fell about in laughter. What followed was extremely moving. The staff affirmed the head in a very beautiful way. Once the hilarity had died down the head lit a candle and asked his staff for forgiveness. In turn many of the staff brought their worries and desire to be forgiven to the community.

The staff then said the Lord's Prayer together and very wisely the head said, 'Our staff meeting has ended. Let us go together in peace to love one another as the Lord Jesus Christ has shown us how to do.'

No one was embarrassed or uncomfortable. Why? Because the sharing and prayer-time were deeply meaningful and *real*. It is this kind of experience that really bonds a staff. These are moments that cannot be contrived or forced: they happen . . . they challenge each of us and if we respond to them they lead into avenues that we never dreamed possible.

Rooted in teaching, worship and moral values

Our religious education must form the *core* of the curriculum. It is the starting point which opens out right across the whole school experience as well as the taught curriculum. It is rooted in three aspects, namely teaching, worship and moral values, and all three are essential components of a whole. If our children are to receive a balanced education in their faith, each must be treated with equal importance.

A word about doctrine: doctrine is the teaching of the Church. The word comes from the Latin word for teaching, and all through this book where the word 'teaching' is used you can substitute the word 'doctrine'.

Teaching means what the Catholic Church believes and teaches to be true.

Worship means how a primary school community celebrates and expresses what it is — what it believes about who God is and the world in which it lives.

Moral values means that, because of what we believe to be true and the way in which we express this, we are called to behave throughout our lives according to Catholic moral values.

The following drawings show how these areas are present in the development of the children's education and how they interrelate with the whole curriculum.

1 How RE grows from teaching, worship and values, and how it is the centre and lifeblood of the curriculum. RE is the heart of the entire curriculum of the Catholic school.

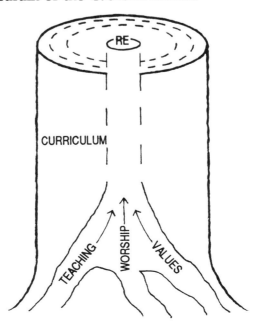

2 How this happens at every age group.

Each horizontal section through the trunk represents the areas of experience gained by the pupils through the taught curriculum in a year. It also represents the effect on the pupil of the organization of the school, and the attitudes and values of the staff and the actions which result (the hidden curriculum).

The height of each slice represents the progression which is aimed at in each area of experience during that year.

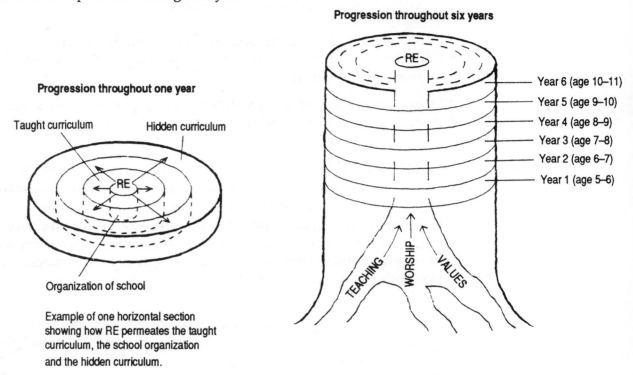

Progression throughout one year

Taught curriculum   Hidden curriculum

RE

Organization of school

Example of one horizontal section showing how RE permeates the taught curriculum, the school organization and the hidden curriculum.

Progression throughout six years

RE

Year 6 (age 10–11)
Year 5 (age 9–10)
Year 4 (age 8–9)
Year 3 (age 7–8)
Year 2 (age 6–7)
Year 1 (age 5–6)

TEACHING   WORSHIP   VALUES

3 How RE interacts with the rest of the curriculum including the hidden curriculum (which is what children learn from the atmosphere and attitudes of the school which may contradict what they learn in lessons).

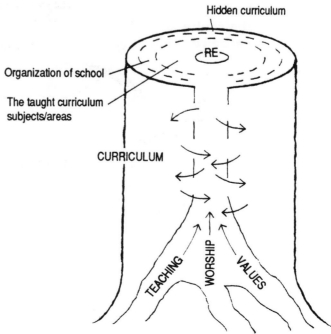

Hidden curriculum

Organization of school

The taught curriculum subjects/areas

RE

CURRICULUM

TEACHING   WORSHIP   VALUES

The Church's liturgical year

By using the ancient tradition of the liturgical year as a framework, we can draw on the wealth of the whole Church to teach our children who God is and what they are.

What we are saying is that all education is religious because it is about discovering

- the uniqueness and dignity of individuals
- where they have come from
- what are the challenges and discoveries that now face them
- the mysteries and wonders of God's world and how they can be enjoyed and fathomed.

Whatever area of exploration the pupils are engaged in, it is all about discovering the mysteries and wonders of life.

We are all part of God's creation

When we say that God is the centre of our life, then this must be experienced by our whole community in some way, even by the very youngest. It isn't a case of dragging God or religion into everything we do — God is already there. What we are doing is looking at education as God's work.

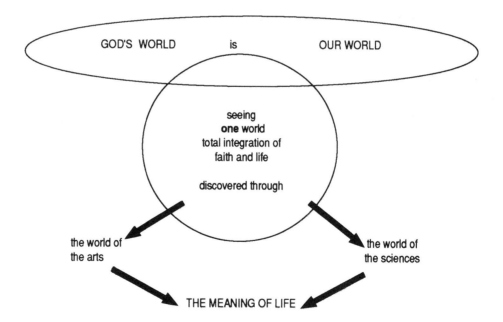

19

Being a eucharistic community: the school eucharist

It is often difficult for teachers to say what they mean when asked to explain how the school is a eucharistic community. What one hears so often is:

      'Mass is very important in our school.'

or   'We have Mass here every week.'

or   'Every class has a class Mass each half-term.'

but when one probes deeper and asks the question — how does this affect your life in this community and how does it affect the life of the children? — it becomes very difficult for teachers to give an answer.

Many primary schools are now experiencing something which has long been known in secondary schools, and that is pupils saying 'Mass is boring!'

Ever younger children now echo this chorus. The reasons for this situation are many and complex, as I discovered from recent discussions with teachers.

The infant class teachers expressed the greatest concern. They felt their children were excluded by language and symbol, by not being able to receive communion, and by having to sit still or concentrate for what is for them a long time. At first it seemed that Mass for the under-sevens was *out*. Teachers could find no meaningful way for our infants to participate in even one major part of our celebrations, until one person asked the question, 'What are our children capable of at that age?' The school gate provided a key insight.

I happened to be in a reception class at 3.15 p.m. The teacher and welfare assistant both moved with great skill and dexterity as they placed eighteen coats the right way up on eighteen little bodies, did up buttons in the correct order, had everyone lined up and, with the welfare assistant bringing up the rear, lined everyone up for the moment the bell rang out to signal the 'off'.

What happened was fascinating. Only able to watch two children closely, I observed their mothers untangle themselves from the school gate to greet their offspring as they rushed towards them waving pictures of their latest discoveries and paper hats to show that they now knew the colour green.

Both mothers had shopping — both had other children. What I had expected was the mothers to attach the pupils to themselves via the pushchair or a hand, but no. One mother took the fragile picture and green hat and carefully placed them in a carrier bag and then handed the pushchair over to our little student. He had a task and a big responsibility to carry out: pushing the baby home. This helpless reception pupil now became Mummy's 'big boy' who helped and *was* a help.

Our second child received the same reception from her mother and then took the hand of her little sister to walk home with her.

What interested me was that her mother allowed the five-year-old to assume this responsibility whilst she pushed a pushchair full of shopping, painting and green paper hat!

The lesson is one we all know but seldom really take seriously. When children come to us at four or five, they are very young. But they come with skills, with some education and a certain amount of responsibility. They are Mummy's 'big boy or girl'. They are not (usually) babyfied. They are expected to help and take responsibility. The question for us is how far do we — or does the system — allow for development or do we in fact de-skill to a certain degree? This same situation is painfully evident at the secondary level.

Over the past four years, we have gained many insights into children's understanding of celebration — and appropriate ways of celebrating being a eucharistic people and community. It is these that we wish to share.

Access is a key issue. Language and symbolism are major areas. We must ask the questions:

• is the language being used suitable for the group?
• are the symbols relevant and meaningful for the age group?

Expectations: are we being reasonable in what we expect of the age group taking part in this celebration?

Participation: can everyone identify and join in with what is happening? Is there a part for them?

Experience: can this group relate this celebration to their life? Is it meaningful?

Although it is most important that the whole school community experiences good celebrations of the eucharist, it is equally important that we do not rush into expecting very young children to understand and participate in what is essentially a very adult celebration. The eucharist is such a complex celebration that we need to rediscover the depth and richness of each part and not be afraid to celebrate each section with the children one step at a time.

We have allocated a section of the eucharist to each year group:

This has been specially linked to the overall content of the syllabus for that year group. However, it is important that schools feel quite free to adjust the eucharistic themes to fit their own needs.

As professionals in the art of teaching young children we applied all our teaching skills to the challenge of helping our young community *experience the eucharist at their level.* The following is *a way* of doing this.

YEAR 1 GATHERING

Welcome celebrations

Year 1, the first full class in the infant school, will vary in age range according to your admissions policy. The following suggestions recognize that some children will be under five years old. Where there is a separate reception class teachers will be able to share Year 1 activities with them.

Building on the 'school gate' experience, our Year 1 children are the people responsible for calling the community to worship. They gather us all together and welcome everyone. They lead us in this part of the eucharistic celebration.

Throughout their year in this class, the pupils will experience many celebrations of 'gathering' and 'welcome'.

First step: preparing a special place for people to come to in the classroom.

Second step: placing the special story book (the Bible) in a central position where everyone can see it. Explain to the children that this book is something very holy and we all have to take care of it. It has a beautiful cover. Inside is the most wonderful story in the world, the story of how much God loves each one of us.

Third step: the call to gather. This could be through voice, song or through the sound of instruments. Special people are chosen for a week to be the ones to call the class to the place for gathering, a place to be happy together because each person is one of God's own children, loved and unique.

An example of a simple ceremony

The *call* is heard:
— musical instrument sounds
— children gather with staff around the special book
— candle is lit
— flowers are placed to add to beauty

Talk about how good it is to be together with all our friends.
Sing Gathering song.
Join hands in circle around the Bible.
Look at the candle and the book.

Make a sign of how much we love each other — a hug, kiss, handshake.
Say a sentence saying how happy we are to be together with each other and with Jesus.

Widening the celebration to other classes

As the children become accustomed to the format of
— the call to gather
— carrying the special book
— gathering and celebrating
you can begin to talk about other people in the school.

Start with other infant classes. Widen their experience of calling and gathering by sending people to call another class — each person bringing someone whom they are going to sit down with and look after.

Parents

These celebrations can also take place at the end of the day to include parents and friends who have come to collect the children.

The children go to the school gate and gather their parents into their special place for celebration.

Four- or five-year-olds who know exactly what is expected of them, when and where to go are usually pretty determined in the carrying out of their duties. No adult will be allowed to dither or delay!

It is essential that all the children know exactly what is expected and what they are responsible for.

YEAR 2   THE WORD

Listening to God speaking to us

The children are now well used to gathering around the special story book and understand that it is something to be treasured. They have experienced how important the Bible is by seeing it in its special place and learning to carry it in procession for celebrations as a class and for the big school celebrations.

This year they are going to learn more about the stories contained in it and discover that it is a way in which God can speak to them.

Words are very exciting for children who are just beginning to read. One important lesson for the children to learn is that the words they learn can be used in two ways:

> to make people happy
> or
> to make people sad.

When God speaks to us through his special book, it is always to help us and make us happy.

1 Celebrating God's Word — using the Old Testament

Gather the children around the Bible.

Sing a Gathering song as you place seven *unlit* candles around the Bible.

Explain to the children that we are now going to hear some of the great stories from the Bible and discover the meaning of some of these special words.

Explain that the Bible is like their reading area. It contains many smaller books. Their first celebration is going to be focused on the first story in the first book.

GENESIS

Tell the first story of how God made the world, stressing the words 'God said . . .' and that when God spoke words what happened was very good.

Or read the following story, with the children repeating the chorus '*And it was very good*' after each part. This story has been laid out on separate sheets so that it can be photocopied for the children.

As an alternative you can read 'The World Is Good' from *Listen*, page 14, and let the children repeat the same chorus.

Our beautiful world

God is full of so much love that he wanted to share that he decided to make our beautiful world.

(light candle 1)

God wanted to make a world full of wonderful things, so he said: 'Let there be dry land and let it be called Earth.'
And so it was.
And it was very good.

(light candle 2)

God looked at the dry land and decided that it needed something different around it — something different from dry — so he made wet and said: 'Let it be called sea and oceans.'
And so it was.
And it was very good.

(light candle 3)

Then God looked at the dry land and the wet seas and decided that this was not enough. They needed something to go all the way around them — so he spoke again and said: 'Let there be a beautiful heaven above the dry land and the wet seas and let it be called the sky.'
And so it was.
And it was very good.

(light candle 4)

And the sky wrapped itself around the beautiful dry land and the wet seas. God saw that something more was still needed — something that would always shine and show the beauty of the dry earth, the wet seas and the beautiful skies. And so God said: 'Let there be a brilliant light in the sky during the day. And soft sparkling lights in the sky by night.' And so God created the Sun for the day and the stars and the Moon for the night.
And so it was.
And it was very good.

(light candle 5)

Now God looked hard at all his work, but still there was more to do — the dry earth needed things in it, the wet seas seemed too big with nothing in them and the bright skies looked so empty and lonely.

So God created plants and trees to grow in the dry land.
Fish and sea creatures for the wet seas.
And beautiful, graceful birds to fly in the skies.
And so it was.
And it was very good.

(light candle 6)

But still God felt there was something missing. He looked at the beautiful dry land full of brightly coloured flowers and plants, the deep blue-green seas with fish and sea creatures of every kind, the vast heavens above carrying birds of every kind and he said: 'My beautiful world needs lots of people to live in it and to be happy.'
And so he made us — boys and girls, men and women.
And so it was.
And it was very good.

(light candle 7)

And so God looked at his beautiful world filled with
       Earth and seas
       Sky and Sun
       Moon and stars
       Plants, animals and birds
       Fish and sea creatures
       Boys and girls
(All together)
And it was very, very good.

2 Listening to God speaking to us (New Testament)

Gather again around the Bible. Explain that the books inside the Bible are in two parts:

- stories before Jesus was born
- stories about Jesus and the time after he was born.

The children have looked at the first book of the Bible, Genesis, and now they are going to look at the first book of the second half of the Bible, Matthew, to find something very special that Jesus said about little children (Matthew 19:13–15).

One day Jesus was very busy talking to grown-ups and they were talking and talking. Some grown-ups were trying to get close to Jesus with their children so that they could talk to him. But the children kept getting pushed back or sent away. The children were getting very upset because no one would let them see Jesus. And when you are very small, what can you do with all these noisy grown-ups?

Suddenly Jesus spotted his friends pushing the children away and telling them not to be a nuisance and go away because the grown-ups were talking about important matters — nothing to do with children. Suddenly Jesus called out in a loud voice:

'Hey, leave the children alone — they are my friends too and very important. Move back, you grown-ups, and let them through.' The children were so pleased because they knew that their friend Jesus would not send them away because he loved them.

Then he did something which really silenced all the grown-ups. He gathered all the children really close to him — put one on his knee and said:

'Never stop children from coming to see me — I love them very much and they will all be with me in heaven one day because they are so good and very beautiful.'

He gave them a hug and blessed them. The grown-ups were speechless.

Play some quiet, reflective music.

Invite the children to sit or lie down in a comfortable position.

Ask the children to close their eyes and imagine they are one of the children trying to get to Jesus:

(1) What does it feel like not to be able to get through a crowd of big people? (Share thoughts or leave silent)

(2) Imagine you are very near Jesus and you're just about to say 'hello' when someone shouts at you to go away. How do you feel?

(3) Now you hear Jesus calling you to come up to him. He picks you up — tells the grown-ups off for not letting you get to him. How do you feel now, sitting on his knee?

(4) What would you say to him?

(5) What do you think he would say back?

Allow the class time really to imagine each scene — either keep it as a silent meditation or allow a sharing of thoughts each time.

Sing a song about talking to Jesus.

Jesus, let me tell you

A song about talking to Jesus - Year 2

© Deirdre Madeley 1991

YEAR 3   RECONCILIATION

Showing we love each other by saying sorry

Listening to God speaking to us through the great stories of the Bible in Year 2 has prepared the way for the children now to respond to these words. Before we can respond fully it is necessary to see what we might need to put right in our daily lives. Celebration of Reconciliation should be a normal and natural part of our daily living and not something restricted to Advent or Lent or just before we prepare for First Holy Communion.

The children will vary greatly in their maturity and ability to understand the difference between right and wrong. The examples which follow are all rooted in the children's daily experience and should not present any problems for those members of the class who still have difficulties in this area.

When something happens in the daily life of the children it is always much more effective to celebrate saying sorry as soon as possible. Ideally it should be a natural part of putting things right whenever necessary. Then the children learn very quickly that it is through their liturgy and prayer that real reconciliation can come about.

Using water to say sorry

With the children select a suitable water container, large enough for every one to see clearly and, if desired, to place their hands in. You will also need a hand towel for the children to dry their hands on afterwards.

Gather the children into a circle around the water and the towel. Place a lighted candle by the water. Explain to the children that when we gather in this way we are doing something exciting and special. The candle is there to remind us of special occasions, happy times when we are with people we love, like birthday parties, special meals or reunions.

Talk about a time when something happened in your own life or a recent experience of the class that made everyone feel unhappy.

Spend time talking about how people felt when this happened.
Sad . . . unhappy . . . wanting to go home . . . lonely . . . wishing it had not happened . . . wishing to say sorry . . . Try to end the sharing on *wanting to be friends again.*

Talk about water with the class, how it gives life and refreshes us when we are tired. Link this in with their feelings and yours when you feel unhappy because of hurting someone else or being upset yourself.

Invite some of the class, one at a time, to immerse their hands in the water and as they do it say how it feels. Invite the person sitting next to them to dry their friend's hands very gently. Ask the person drying the hands of their friend how they feel about this. (They are happy to help, to do something kind.)

Discuss the cleansing qualities of water and the way in which it makes things clean.

Draw out the link between giving life, refreshing and making clean and what Jesus wants us to do when something goes wrong. He wants us to be forgiving and forgiven. To be refreshed and as good as new again! When we place our hand in the water we say:

'Jesus, I love you very much. I want to love everyone in my class. Help me always to love everyone.'

Light the candle, lift it high into the air and gently bring the end of the lighted candle down into the water. As you do this tell the children that the water is now going to be blessed and made holy for our celebration of love and forgiveness.

'Jesus, light of the world, bless this special water that we are going to use to show our love for you and each other. In the name of the Father and of the Son and of the Holy Spirit.'

As the blessing is pronounced, make the sign of the cross over the water. Place the candle beside the bowl but out of harm's way!

In turn each child places his or her hands in the water and turns to the person next to them to be dried. As this is being done, the class says the prayer : *'Jesus, I love you...'*

When this is completed a sign of peace is shared, handshake, hug, etc.

After using this special water it is important not just to throw it away. The children have understood that it is holy and special. Discuss with the class what should be done with the water. How can it be used to continue to give life and refresh something else? (Pour on plants in special nature area.) This should be done seriously and carefully as it now has a particular meaning for each person who has taken part in the celebration.

A suitable song ends the celebration.

Thank you, Lord

YEAR 4   OFFERTORY

Sharing God's gifts to us with everyone

The children in Year 4 now have a good grasp of what it is to be a member of a community, and their need to relate to one another. Through their special study in Year 2 of 'The Word' they have been introduced to some of the fundamental principles of being a member of this Christian community. Now as we concentrate our thoughts on the Offertory and the idea of giving without counting the cost, we are bringing the children into a deeper understanding of this part of the eucharist.

This means a deeper understanding of what it means to:
     (a) be gifted
     (b) be a gift for one another
     (c) share gifts
     (d) see Jesus as a gift to us
     (e) share gifts of bread and wine.

Each of these aspects can be developed into a separate liturgy and with variations be re-celebrated throughout the year.

Celebrating my gifts

Gather the children together around the Word. Light a candle and place it beside the Word. Talk about what we mean when we say someone is 'gifted'. What do they think their gifts are? Hold a class discussion about gifts they see in one another.

Ask each child to think about the gift they treasure the most. Allow the children a few moments to think about this special gift. Give each child a piece of paper and coloured pencils, and ask them, through drawing, prose, poetry or a combination of all three, to illustrate this gift that God has given them. Bring the drawings back to the reflection area and lay them around the table of the Word.

Ask each child in turn just to name their gift in a simple prayer of thanksgiving, e.g. *'Thank you Jesus for the gift of being able to play the piano'* or *'Thank you Jesus for the gift of a sense of humour'*.

This idea can be further developed by allowing the children to demonstrate their gifts more fully either individually or in groups. As each child concludes their demonstration the whole class joins in singing the 'Thank you for our gifts' song.

To be a gift for one another

This celebration concentrates on the aspects of kindness, generosity and love for one another as being great gifts that we can share.

Gather the children around the Word and the lighted candle. Talk about the many times that Jesus loved people and showed this love through friendship even to the point of crying when those he loved were ill or had died.

Give each child a piece of paper about the size of a page of this book. Cut the paper into two pieces lengthwise. Measure to make a headband to fit each child. Staple the two pieces together to create one long strip. Ask each child to think about words that represent the gifts of love, kindness and friendship. The children write or draw illustrations of these words on their long strips and colour the whole strip. When completed, staple to form a headband.

Gather the children back into the reflection area and allow them, one at a time, to talk about the words that they have chosen. As they finish their explanation they are invited to wear their headbands.

Conclude the celebration by singing the song 'Give me joy in my heart', replacing the word 'joy' in each verse with some of those selected and displayed on the headbands.

Sharing gifts

For this celebration it is necessary to spend a few moments thinking about sharing things that we value. For many children this is extremely difficult. Invite the children each to bring something that they really like to play with. These toys will form part of our celebration.

Talk about the risks of sharing something:
— It might be damaged.
— It might be lost.
— It might not be given back.
— We might not want to share it.
— We might only want to share it with our best friends.

Tell the story from the Bible of how Jesus says, 'Whatever you do to the least of my brothers and sisters, you do to me'. Talk about what that means.

Ask each child to talk about their favourite toy and why they like it so much. As each child finishes speaking ask the group if there is anyone who would really like to play with that toy. When each child has finished allow the children to go in groups to share their toys, remembering all the things that we have talked about and how difficult it is sometimes to share. After about 15 minutes bring the groups back, lay the toys around the Bible and the lighted candle and invite the children to make their own prayer, thanking God for the fun that they have just had and the joy of sharing.

Jesus as a gift for us

In this celebration we will concentrate on the theme of the gift of Jesus' friendship. Gather the children around the Word, placing small votive candles in a semi-circle around the Bible. (These can easily be obtained from your local church.)

Talk about the feelings that the children have about Jesus and the kind of person they think that he is. What sort of a friend is he to them?

Give each child a piece of paper and ask them to draw or write down what kind of a friend Jesus is for them, e.g.

Invite the children to bring these thoughts back to the reflection area. As each child shares his or her thoughts with the group, another child lights one of the votive candles.

End the celebration with a song on friendship.

Gifts of bread and wine

This celebration would best be held at the end of a detailed project on bread and wine but a simplified version can be just as effective.

Invite the children to bring in as many different kinds of bread as possible. Talk about ways in which it is made and all the many different varieties. Explain to the children that bread is part of our staple diet.

If there is time, allow the children to make some simple leavened bread. The ingredients you need are strong flour, yeast, sugar, salt and water. Explain the characteristics of each ingredient:

Yeast

This is an organism which grows, given the right conditions. These are warmth (warm water) and food (sugar). The yeast gives off a gas, carbon dioxide, which, when the dough is kneaded, becomes trapped and allows the bread to rise.

'The kingdom of heaven is like the yeast a woman took and mixed with three measures of flour till it was leavened all through.' Matthew 13:33

Flour

This is the basic ingredient and contains gluten which, when wet and kneaded, becomes elastic, like clay.

'Like clay in the potter's hand, so you are in mine.' Jeremiah 18:6

Sugar

This is the food supply for the yeast.

'Its taste was like that of wafers made of honey.' Exodus 16:31

Water

This binds everything together.

'The water that I shall give him will become in him a spring of water, welling up for eternal life.' John 4:14

Salt

Salt brings out and strengthens the flavour of the mixture.

'Salt is a good thing, but if salt has become insipid, how can you make it salty again?' Mark 9:50

Bread recipe

Ingredients
1 lb (450g) flour
1 tsp (5ml) salt
1/2 oz (15g) yeast
1 tsp (5ml) sugar
1/2–2/3 pt (300–400 ml) water

Mix flour and salt. Mix yeast and sugar with 1/4 pt (150 ml) of warm water. Leave in warm place for 10 mins or so to froth up. Pour liquid into flour and then gradually add rest of water. Mix well. Put dough in greased and warmed bread tin and leave in warm place, covered with a cloth, for 20 mins to rise. Bake at 200°C/400°F/Gas Mark 6 for 35-40 mins.

Lay out all the necessary ingredients. Talk about each one in turn. Ask the children, after they have heard what each ingredient is for, to see if they can unravel or discover the mystery of why bread is so often used as a symbol in the Bible.

Jesus said, 'I am the bread of life'

Allow each child to make some bread. Whilst the bread is baking invite the class to think about someone at home, or at school, that they would like to give their bread to. Each child can make a special basket for their bread out of coloured paper and decorate the side of the basket with the words 'Jesus said, I am the bread of life'. When the bread is baked and cooled and put in the baskets, gather the baskets together and place them around the table of the Word. Light the candle and invite each child to pray for his or her special person.

Sing a bread and gifts song.

I am the vine — you are the branches

For this part of the celebration you will need some grapes, some grape juice and a vine branch.

You may want to spend some time in studying the symbolism of grapes and wine in scripture before going into the celebration with bread.

When the children have placed their bread in the oven to bake and returned to the reflection area, lay beside the candle a bunch of grapes and, if possible, a vine branch. Place beside the grapes an empty chalice or goblet.

Give each child a grape to hold gently in their hand. Ask them to eat the grape quietly, slowly, and carefully. Invite each member of the class to try and describe what the grape tasted like.

Discuss with the children why Jesus drank wine at meals. Point out that in the country where Jesus lived, like France or Spain, wine was a common table drink and not as special as it is here, because it was much cheaper and even poor people could afford it.

Place the vine branch and the remaining grapes back beside the candle. Invite one of the children to read the scripture verses from St John's Gospel about the vine.

Talk about this and ask the children what they think it means. Can they see now why Jesus said 'I am the vine — you are the branches'?

End this part of the celebration by pouring some grape juice for each child to drink.

Concluding prayer: Jesus help us to stay as close to you as the branches are to the vine. Thank you for the gifts of bread and wine.

YEAR 5 BREAKING THE BREAD

Celebrating sharing our love around the table of sacrifice

One of the problems which we have to overcome, when trying to deepen the children's understanding about meals and the place of the table in worship, is that for many of them sharing a meal around a table is a rare event. Many of our young children do not sit down to a family meal more than once or twice a week. We need to begin in the daily experience of our children. For five days of each week, the children have a midday meal with us. For most this is far from a holy or dignified occasion. Many of our children rush through eating their food with the sole aim of getting out of the dining room as fast as possible. Is it any surprise to us that, when we try to tell our pupils the eucharist is a meal where people celebrate being together and sharing in the food of the bread and wine, this imagery fails to excite, or even interest, most of them?

The structure of our meal times is crucial. What follows is just one way of tackling this challenge.

Divide the school into family groupings for meal times; where possible have the whole age range represented at each table.

Talk with the class about the experiences they have during school dinner-time. Ask them to think of ways in which they could improve the following:
(a) the environment
(b) lay-out of individual tables, making them look attractive
(c) conversation
(d) prayer
(e) table manners
(f) helping younger children
(g) showing that we really care about everyone.

Assign an area of responsibility to each age group.

Year 6 to befriend and look after Reception and Year 1. This will mean collecting them from their classroom and taking them to their special place in the dining room, having them sit next to the Year 6 person at the table. These pupils are also responsible for behaviour at the table and seeing that everyone is attentive to the needs of their neighbour. It will be necessary to watch that the youngest and slowest eaters are not unnecessarily rushed.

Year 5 to be responsible for decorating the table and laying it.

Year 4 to be responsible for the conversation topic each week. This could be assisted by asking a different person each day to bring something special they have done in class to tell the others about. They could also talk about their homes, brothers and sisters, etc. But the topic of the conversation will be introduced and led by the person from Year 4.

Year 3 to be responsible for designing and making a special place mat for everyone at their table. This could form a useful technology exercise as well. This tablemat could be laminated so that it is not spoilt.

Year 2 to be responsible for the prayers before and after each meal. These can be very simple and spontaneous.

It is important that the children actually experience waiting until everyone is seated before praying together, then, whether they're having hot dinners or sandwiches, nobody begins to eat until everyone at the table has food before them. It is also important to teach the children to wait until everyone has finished before clearing away. Their final act is to pray together in thanksgiving for their food and friendship.

All of these responsibilities can be rotated between the different classes.

From this the children learn that it is important to see our meal times as more than a time for just consuming food. They are a time for sharing who we are as people, as brothers and sisters, who care for and love each other. Gathering together for a meal is something special. It is a happy time. It is a holy time. It is a time to renew and refresh our whole being.

If the community approaches a meal time in this spirit it is consistent with what we teach and claim that we practise: when we say we are a eucharistic people, we are saying that we are a people for whom table fellowship is extremely important. Our children need to experience this as the norm, not as the exception.

This pattern can be introduced to the school by Year 5 with the help of their class teacher. Small groups can explain the different responsibilities to each year group.

The staff as a whole will need to meet with the headteacher, to discuss the logistics and individual preparation that each year group will need to do. You will find that the children will quickly respond very positively to their new responsibilities and take them seriously. It is important that the staff give the children time to prepare properly. Not only are the children experiencing meals in a very different way. They are also learning to listen to children of all ages, to hold a conversation at a table and to be understanding and tolerant of one another. The Year 6 children will take on a big responsibility in seeing that the table manners and general behaviour are of the highest standard. There will need to be some preparation beforehand with the reception class teacher, about ways in which they can help the youngest children to handle cutlery and join in the sharing at the table. A Year 6 child can also take the responsibility of being the daily monitor or prefect over the whole dining room. Their task would be to see that the children went a table at a time for their hot dinners and, in the event of the Year 6 pupil being absent for the day, seeing that a Year 5 pupil took over the responsibility for a table. They would also see that the tables were left cleared and clean at the end of the meal.

Meal celebrations in the classroom

There are many meal stories in the New Testament and they provide an excellent background for celebrations of this kind in the classroom.

Invite the children to bring some of their favourite foods in for a special meal. Stress that these are things that they really like to eat and drink.

Divide into working groups to undertake the following responsibilities:

(1) setting out a table and laying it
(2) making a list of all the food and setting it out
(3) choosing one of the meal stories from scripture and preparing a play to be acted out at the meal
(4) preparing some music to be sung or played at the meal to act as a prayer
(5) making special place names
(6) making some flower arrangements or decorations for the table.

Everyone is invited to hand their food to the group setting it out. This is arranged on big plates in the middle of the table.

When everyone is seated the group responsible for the music and prayer begins the meal celebrations.

It is then explained to everyone seated at the table that all may eat freely but only the food that someone else *offers them*. They may not eat anything that they take for themselves! This may well cause some consternation! Recall again the celebrations on gifts and sharing that they had in their previous class. Remember why we are having this meal. We are remembering what Jesus did when he gave everything for us. This little sharing is a symbol for us. In laying on the table food and drink that we really want to take back again and eat ourselves, we know, in a little way, what it feels like to make a sacrifice. Stress that everyone needs to be attentive to their neighbours, who may not ask for any particular food and must eat what is placed before them, so don't give them too much. When everyone has eaten enough, the group who have prepared the play perform it for the whole class. A discussion may follow. The music group ends the celebration by leading everybody in a song or prayer.

Some useful texts

Matthew 9:10-13	Luke 5:29-32	John 12:1-11
Matthew 14:13-21	Luke 10:38-42	John 13:1-20
Matthew 15:32-39	Luke 14:1-24	John 21:9-14
Matthew 26:6-13	Luke 24:36-43	
Matthew 26:17-19		
Matthew 26:26-29		

YEAR 6 THANKSGIVING

Celebrating saying 'Thank you'

This theme is especially important for the Year 6 children. This is their final year in the school. During the year they will be reflecting on all that they have learnt and experienced in their time with you. At each stage of their reflection they will be giving thanks for things learnt, for people they have known and loved, for the times they have been forgiven and for the ability to forgive. They will give thanks for everyone who has helped them to come to this stage in their life. Their final celebration, sending forth and saying goodbye, brings the year to a climax. This will be their last opportunity to say 'thank you' themselves and to hear their community return their thanks. The following are a few ideas for highlighting some of these aspects during the year.

'Thank you' for my friends

By the time the pupils reach Year 6 they know one another very well. They have been through a lot together. Gather the class together in their reflection area and ask them to think about a time when they really valued someone in the class, especially someone that they don't normally play with. Talk about these times. Ask for someone in the class to read out very slowly the names of everyone in the class, pausing for a few moments after each name for reflection. Think about each one in turn and imagine what you might like to say to them that was good and encouraging and a thank you.

Give each child a large sheet of paper. Ask them to return to their places and write their name neatly at the top of the page and then to leave their pen beside the paper and return to the reflection area in silence. After a few minutes tell them to go to any desk, sit down silently and write a good thing which they thought about that person in the quiet time that they have just had. Each child should go to every desk in turn. They can begin with the words 'I would like to thank you . . .' Play some quiet music and tell the class that there is no rush. They should take their time and write from the heart. It is important that there is a paper for the teacher too and that the teacher writes something on each pupil's paper. This exercise is done in silence and as each person finishes they return to the reflection area to sit silently.

When everybody has finished and all are seated back in the reflection area, the children will be very excited to see what has been written. To protect confidentiality it is important that the teacher gather up all the papers before the children see them.

The children are now invited to make a card out of another piece of paper folded in half, with suitable words on the outside, e.g: 'Thank you Jesus for . . . (name of friend)'. Whilst the class are making cards, quickly check through the thank-you papers for any inappropriate remarks. As each child finishes the card for their friend they return with their card to the reflection area. The children are invited to exchange cards and they are then given their own thank-you papers to read and place inside the card that their friend has made.

As each child receives their paper, remember that this may be the first time for many of them that people have really expressed so many positive comments about them. You will find yourself quite moved by what the children say to you.

Light the candle and sing a thank-you song together for the wonderful gift of friends.

'Thank you' for all I have learnt

For this celebration you will need a thurible or small fireproof container, a piece of incense charcoal and some grains of incense.

Gather the children into the reflection area and talk about the length of time that they have been together.

Ask them to think about the things that they have learnt and become good at that they value the most. What are they most pleased that they have learnt? Share these in the group.

Place a lighted candle and the thurible in the middle of the group. Explain to the children that today they will be using incense to help them pray. Give each member of the class a grain of incense and place it in the palm of their hand. Take the piece of charcoal and light it. Place it in the thurible. The charcoal is fully alight when it turns grey. Explain to the group that this special area of knowledge and skills, which they value the most, has been given them by God. At the moment they have just begun the process of understanding it. They now have the task of fanning this little flame of knowledge into something much bigger. Ask them to look at the grain of incense. How small it is. It's a bit like the knowledge they have at the moment, but when they place it on the burning charcoal it will be transformed and changed into something which will affect the whole room. The little grain of incense represents the gift that they have been given. Only they can place it on the charcoal.

Invite each child to name the area of knowledge that they want to thank God for and then place their grain of incense on the charcoal.

When all have placed their incense on the charcoal draw their attention to the incense rising up and permeating the whole atmosphere. Point out to them that this is what God has called them to do and given them the gifts to do it with. If they use their gifts properly they will be like the incense, filling every corner of the room. This is what we thank God for.

Sing a thank-you song.

Throughout the year each class group is focusing on one aspect of the eucharist. It is very important that when the school comes together for a full eucharistic celebration each part of the eucharist should be celebrated to the full and led by that age group. In this way our children are playing a much fuller part and are able to understand and benefit to a greater extent from this complete celebration.

This will mean that your school celebrations of the eucharist can no longer be fitted into forty minutes or an hour. To do so would be to contradict what we have been teaching the children about the wealth of meaning within each part. Our schools have never found a problem with keeping the children enthusiastically involved when the eucharist is celebrated in full. The eucharist may well take most of a morning or an afternoon, but how much better it is when the celebration is a deep and meaningful experience that children can look forward to with excitement.

Part 2

EXAMPLES OF WHOLE-SCHOOL CELEBRATIONS

These are examples of whole-school celebrations: further whole-school celebrations for Giving thanks, All Souls and All Saints, Advent, Candlemas and Lent will appear in the forthcoming primary course *The Rainbow People*.

In the planning of each celebration consideration should be given to ways of inviting the involvement of parents and parish. Spaces have been added to the planning charts to encourage discussion about how this may be done.

In each celebration there is a range of activities for Year 1 from which an appropriate role can be chosen for the reception class.

Welcome

How our children are initiated into their school community is extremely important. Children need a sense of identity, of who they are and where they come from. They need to know that they are Christians in the Catholic tradition. The whole of their lived experience in the school community should in some way help them to develop this identity.

The welcome theme is designed not just for the new children coming into your school but for everyone who is beginning in this new situation, teachers, welfare assistants, governors, parents and friends. Preparation for this theme will need to begin in the second half of the summer term.

The first point you may need to consider and articulate is 'What are these new people being welcomed to?'

This will lead to the next question, 'What are we doing when we welcome people into our community?'

It is necessary to look at the whole school environment and see how the theme of welcome can be reinforced and expressed in different ways, right across the life of the school and the curriculum. The following areas are suggested as a plan for doing this. It is important to remember that this plan must be adapted and expanded to fit your particular needs. It is envisaged that this theme would not be completed in one or two days but would last for several days, to enable each area to be fully developed in an unrushed and exciting way. You will notice that each of the six areas can be expanded to go into other curriculum areas. What is important is that by the time the community reaches the celebration stage they are feeling very much at home and at ease in their new school community.

ENVIRONMENT
Names and pictures of new friends
prepared by children
displayed in school

MY STORY
Building up of personal story
Life in school so far
New people begin story, others continue
Each term another chapter
Faith development

RELATIONSHIPS
Children help welcome new friends
Getting to know one another
Looking after one another

WELCOME

CELEBRATING
Our new friends
Celebration with Sign of Belonging
  BADGE, BIBLE, SWEATER
Parents, teachers, children
recall baptism

SPECIAL PLACES
Classrooms, pegs, lockers, meals,
family groupings

OUR STORY
Who we are as
community
school
in the family of God

TREASURE TRAIL
Finding our way around
New and exciting discoveries

The environment

By the last month of the summer term you will probably have a nearly complete list of your new intake of children. You may not, as yet, have a complete list of helpers or staff. But a start can be made with the present Year 5 (Year 6 in September) in selecting names of new pupils and adults coming to the school in September who could be written to and welcomed.

Example 1: Child's letter

Dear Daniel

My name is David. I have been asked to look after you when you come to our school in September. You are going to be in mr potter's class. He has taught us LOGO on the computer. We are making our own hardback books with marble ink covers. So far mine has got two stories, a poem and a map. Mr potter is calm and very clever. We go swimming every thursday and some of us are going camping in Bayeux next June.

School has got a soccer pitch with flood lights, three halls and loads of computers. please send me a photograph of yourself so I know what you look like. Do you like chess, books, the BEANO. or cycling? I do! If you would like to come and play at my house please phone. I look forward to meeting you and being your friend.

David

The pupils might like to invite the new people to send a photograph of themselves or to draw a picture. These can be used for display purposes. It is suggested that if it is a small intake two pupils adopt a new person to write to. The present Year 6, your school leavers for this year, are invited to prepare welcome boards and displays in prominent parts of the school.

Relationships

Years 5 and 6 are already working together by writing letters and collecting pictures/photos of new friends starting in September. In their letters Year 5 explain to the new people as much as they can about the school through pictures as well as writing; they may like to include a picture or photo of themselves. They explain to the new person that they will be there on the first day of term to welcome them and look after them. This is as necessary for teachers and other staff as it is for pupils. I am sure you can remember the butterflies that you felt with every new school that you entered for the first time. Those of us lucky enough to have enjoyed receiving a letter of welcome from a colleague before our first day know how reassuring and comforting that was, how much better it is for any person coming to your school to have received some form of communication from pupil or staff, simply telling them how pleased they are they're coming and that someone is going to be there especially to look after them.

Special places

It is difficult enough for adults in the first days of a new school to find their way around and discover where everything is kept, and much more so for an infant or primary child. Therefore, to assist our new friends we suggest that Year 3 adopt the task of naming, in both symbol and the written word, all the important places in the school. Special attention should be paid to places where new people hang their coats, keep their belongings, areas of classroom, etc. Large colourful labels that have been carefully worked out, so that the youngest non-reader is able to decipher them, should be displayed in prominent, appropriate places.

Example 2: Labels

Treasure trail

Year 4 might be best suited for this area. So far Welcome displays adorn the school, pictures and names of our new friends are clearly evident, relationships are being built up by established pupils befriending newcomers and special places have been named. But still we need to find our way around. To assist with this Year 4 are encouraged to design a treasure trail. Each point on the treasure trail will be an area that the newcomers need to know, e.g. classroom, peg for coat, dining room, toilet etc. The newcomers explore the treasure trail accompanied by their Year 6 friends who enter into the game with them. A prize can be given to every child as they complete their treasure trail.

Example 3: Specimen treasure trail

DINNER HALL AND GYM   KITCHEN   CLASS 1   STORE   OFFICE   LIBRARY   STAFF ROOM

ENTRANCE

Our story

Some schools are very good about passing on the story of the school community. But all too often the richness which is part of their past is forgotten or becomes lost. Headteachers will have been busy with the seemingly endless initiatives hurled in their direction over the past few years. One of the tasks has been the writing of the Mission Statement. As you laboured long and hard to find some pithy statement that said everything and pleased everyone, you would have been faced with the question 'Who are we as a community, a school in the family of God?'

What is most important of all is that our children know why they have come to your school and not some other very caring Christian school elsewhere. *Why your school?* In the past it was sufficient to say 'Because it is a Catholic school'; we all knew what that meant or we thought we did. Our identity was clear. Now some twenty or thirty years later the world and our church in that world have undergone a tremendous evolution.

Many things have changed and in that process parents are not so sure any more what it is to be a Catholic. The Church itself continually struggles to understand its role for the twenty-first century. We must not be surprised to find ourselves involved in this same process. Your school has a rich history. The following checklists might help you to get back in touch with key moments and prominent people who have prepared the way for you, your staff and your children.

(a)   Why was this school founded?
(b)   When was the school founded and by whom?
(c)   What is the history of the name of your school?
(d)   Who was the first headteacher?
(e)   What did the school originally look like and what big changes have there been in buildings?
(f)   Was there a uniform and what was it like?
(g)   How has the school grown in size?
(h)   Have there been any 'special characters', either staff or pupils, over the years, that people fondly remember?
(i)   Have any famous people been to the school?
(j)   What special achievements has the school become known for?
(k)   Which secondary schools do your children go on to?

As you go through your checklist it will help you to select some of the key stages in the growth of your school community. With your staff you might like to allocate a 'time' in the history of the community, or some aspect of the school, for each class. This will include nursery, infants and juniors. It might be helpful to have a staff meeting to allocate responsibilities and tasks for each teacher and his or her class in early June.

Example 4: Planning sheet for Welcome theme

— Fix a date for the planning meeting for WELCOME.
— Circulate this date to staff.
— With the aid of a planning chart (such as the one below) in the staff room, allocate areas of responsibility.

PLANNING CHART

Year	Summer term preparation	Year	Autumn term activity
Reception		1 and Reception	
1 and Reception		2	
2		3	
3		4	
4		5	
5		6	
6		now left	
Parents		Parents	
Parish		Parish	
Other		Other	

Among the things to consider are:
- preparing the room or area for the Welcome 'story-telling'
- preparing the music
- finding people to take charge of hospitality, inviting and looking after visitors
- checking if you need any special props, costumes, art work or scenery, and if so, getting it/them
- making sure there are people to tidy up after the 'story-telling'
- inviting governors, parents, chaplain, friends of the school.

As each class prepares its part of the story it is important to remember that the summer holidays present us with a big gap between preparation and celebration; therefore, it will be important, especially in the infant school, that the story-telling through narration, pictures, song and mime be very simple so that it can be easily and quickly remembered in the first few days of term.

It is important to involve as many people as possible in the telling of the story, both pupils and staff, but also people from the past who are still living and who may be able to come: past pupils, teachers, chaplains and helpers — anyone who will help us to keep our story alive.

On the day selected for the telling of the story invite parents, and friends from the wider community, to come and join you for this special occasion. You will notice that each year your pupils and staff, as well as parents and friends, will become increasingly conscious of why their school community is there, its history and what it promises for the future. As the children move up they become responsible for the telling of another part of the story.

Programme

1. Welcome from the headteacher.

2. Each age group presents its part of the story.

   Year 1 ....

   Year 2 ....

   Year 3 ....

   Year 4 ....

   Year 5 ....

   Year 6 ....

3. The headteacher explains to the new people that now they are part of the story and next year they will have a part in the telling of the story.

4. Celebration of initiation.

Celebrating

Having told our story, the Welcome theme comes to a climax in a celebration of initiation. It is very important to mark and ritualize the entry of the new children into their formal schooling. Their parents presented them to the church for baptism. They, through the sacrament of baptism, began the process of initiation into the Catholic Christian community.

Now their parents are bringing them to this second stage — their Catholic school — and entrusting them to you and your staff to build on what has already begun. It is a very important moment. Parents, godparents, members of the families and friends should all be invited to take part in this celebration. Here, the headteacher, possibly with the chair of governors, formally welcomes these new families into the educating community. It is a wonderful opportunity to remind the parents of their child's baptism and what they undertook then on behalf of that child. Now the headteacher will join them in their task of bringing their children up in the faith.

Until now your new pupils have not been wearing their school uniform (or badge, if the school does not have a uniform). At this celebration, each child is called forward with their special friend and presented with their new clothing. For the very young children the connection between this and their baptism will not be fully understood, but for the adults and the older children present it is a powerful sign, reminiscent of the white garment at baptism. New adults to the community are also called forward with their special friend and given an appropriate symbol of the school. This might be a sweatshirt, school badge, Bible with the school emblem, etc.

As the children receive their new clothes (or article of clothing if more appropriate), they leave the school hall to change, helped by their friend. They re-enter the assembly to a blessing.

My story

The recording and remembering of each person's experience in the school community is very important. Each child in the school and each adult is encouraged to have a special book in which they record key moments, events and people who have in some way played a significant part in the life of the school. The infant school books would need to be of a different style from the junior books. The infants' books would be based more on colouring, drawing and pictures, along with sticking things in, whereas the junior school books would have a greater scope for written records as well. The books could have a special cover, preferably designed by the pupils themselves. The headteacher, as the leader of the community, might like to give each member of staff a special journal to record their thoughts and reflections in.

The reception teacher might have a special picture and simple message welcoming the child by name, which would be glued to page 1 of the infant journal. These would be kept in a very special place (for their protection) and shared with parents at appropriate moments, if the child so wishes.

As the infants move into the junior school, they take their story book with them but now add to it one that will give greater scope for written expression. They will be encouraged to record prayers learnt, and their own, special moments that they have really enjoyed as they learnt something new about themselves and their faith. Moments, too, of difficulty, sad times and times of loss, as well as the very happy times, should be recorded.

At the end of their time in the primary school they will be encouraged to reflect back over the years and see how their faith has grown through a greater knowledge and understanding, beginning with their first day in the school.

Celebrating Christmas

One of the dilemmas that face every primary school is how to cope with Advent and all that needs to be taught during this four-week period, when the inevitable Christmas nativity play and the weeks of preparation for that take up most of the time before the last few days of term and 'the performance'. Inevitably what happens is that Advent is superficially touched upon and ends up giving way to rehearsals and preparations for the Christmas concert. This is to deny the children, and in fact the whole community, the opportunity to celebrate one of the major seasons of the Church's year, Advent. This means that the Christmas event should not start until the last few days of term.

You will notice in the outline syllabus (pages 77-82) for each year group that during the Advent time there is a great deal of material to be covered and experiences to be celebrated. Most headteachers are very worried about the growing secularization of the Christmas event. It is to redress this imbalance that I would propose the following.

Bring Christmas back

One of the areas we need to address is how to keep our expression of the liturgy meaningful and relevant to young children as well as to their families. In the Catholic community we have the natural forum of the parish. Most of our primary schools are reasonably near to the parish church. We can capitalize on this resource; another resource is our parents, who are willing to be involved in the education and spiritual formation of their children.

School or parish

The following celebrations are designed with a strong emphasis on close links between the home, the school and the parish. To ensure that each celebration fits accurately into the liturgical season of the year we have moved the Christmas event back within its true time span. It is celebrated in four parts:

1.   the last week before Christmas — in school

2.   25 December — in church

3.   6 January — in church or school

4.   2 February — in church or school

Style of play/celebration/presentation

Don't be afraid to use the natural gifts of the parish: allow people to create their own improvised scenes around each of the stories. Although this will need some guidance from an overall director or producer, it is important to allow adults and children together to discuss the scriptures and interpret them. In doing so they will identify very closely with the characters and the story.

Looking at the story

Encourage everyone to enter into their part as if they really had been there, and not be afraid to use their own words instead of the words from scripture or some outdated play.

Scripting the improvised scenes can be done if it will boost the confidence of the group. It is important to remember that this is not a dramatic production, but a reliving of a deeply meaningful event which is part of our faith story. Nobody should be excluded from taking part. The beauty of this kind of play/celebration is that it is very flexible.

Adults will need a little coaxing to take part. It might help if teachers were encouraged to take part themselves, and individual parents approached directly, rather than just give out a general invitation.

If the celebrations are to form part of a eucharist, then they can replace the liturgy of the word. It is equally acceptable to celebrate these events outside a eucharist. For the first year or two, you may have to rely on willing staff, governors and one or two parents, but in time you will find that more and more of the parish will quietly come forward, offering their services in either hidden or more public ways. What is important is not how good you are at singing, acting or speaking in public, but how deeply each person enters into the community celebration. The task of the main director or producer is to find ways to make it possible for people to be involved.

Developing the wider themes of the story

You will see from the syllabus that by Year 6 the pupils will have covered an extensive amount of material under the theme of Christmas. They will have moved from being introduced to the story, its characters and the events that took place, to an understanding of the symbolism contained within the story and on into the themes of justice and wider world dimensions contained in the liturgy at Christmas time. It is important to bring in these aspects of the Christmas story, to show the reasons why Jesus was born, to set the context in history, as well as in our time. Several of our schools found it beneficial to portray the historical Jesus as well as the Jesus who lives and moves among us today. You will notice that in Year 6 the Christmas scene is translated

into terms such as:
Where would Jesus be born?
Who would be his friends?
What would he think of our time?
What would be the reactions of different strata of society today?
The children are asked the question: how would *they* react?

Part 1 — Last week before Christmas: The journey

Parish and school will explore together why Mary and Joseph had to leave Nazareth for Bethlehem. This part of the 'Christmas play' can be enacted in school, replacing the traditional Nativity play. Parents, teachers, older and younger brothers and sisters can all take part.

Suggestions for improvised or scripted scenes

Characters needed: Joseph, Mary and members of their families, neighbours from the same tribe (David), announcer who brings the news that all must go to their ancestral town to be registered, robbers, elders of the tribe who keep everyone in order!

Scenes: The announcement is made. Anger and consternation. Elders get control and preparations begin for the long journey. Problems to be solved about looking after the animals and people who are too ill to travel. Modes of travel. Food needed for journey. People planning the route, and arguments about the best way. Joseph worried about Mary and some of the other women who are expecting babies. Discussion amongst the women about what they will need to take for babies who will be born on the way. The journey begins. Robbers try to attack the group. Arriving in Bethlehem. Consternation at the crowds. Younger members who have run ahead to seek out places for rest tell the group that there is no chance of being able to find anywhere in the town. The women very worried about Mary. Joseph says he will go himself and try to find somewhere to stay, taking Mary with him.

Part 2 — 25 December: The birth of Jesus

This part of the story takes place in the parish church on Christmas Day. Again all age groups are involved. This part deals with the birth of Jesus, the arrival of the shepherds and other friends.

Suggestions for improvised or scripted scenes:

Characters: innkeeper and his wife, passers-by, Mary and Joseph, some of the younger members of the tribe who have accompanied Mary and Joseph to help carry bags, shepherds, animals, angels.

Scenes: Joseph and Mary and little group of helpers comfort Mary in the street after being turned away from every house. Small child pleads with Joseph to try once more. Innkeeper's wife argues with husband about taking Mary and Joseph in. Innkeeper says no and slams the door in Joseph's face. Wife sneaks out back door and whistles to Joseph to follow her into outside building. Child says it's perfect and innkeeper's wife and Joseph help Mary into the outhouse.

Jesus is born. Great excitement amongst the little band. Some rush off to tell the rest of their group. Shepherds out in the fields are discussing the excitement and activity of Bethlehem with all the visitors. They see the young children running to tell their families that Mary has had a baby boy. One shepherd laughs as he says: 'As if there aren't enough people in Bethlehem already!' At that point a stranger appears beside one of the shepherds. They are uneasy and afraid because the stranger looks so different from anyone they've seen before. They notice that although it's the middle of the night, there's a strange light filling the place where they're sitting. The stranger speaks and tells them to follow the little children who will show them where a baby is born who is Christ the Lord. Shepherds call after children to wait for them. They get a little lamb as a present for the child.

Part 3 — 6 January: The Epiphany

Here the celebration can be in the parish church or in the school. This section of the story deals with the arrival of the wise men to pay homage to Jesus.

Suggestions for improvised or scripted scenes

Characters: Wise men, Herod, courtiers, Holy Family, passers-by, children.

Scenes: Wise men resting outside Jerusalem debating what to do now. They agree to seek out the local leader and ask his advice. A passer-by tells the wise men that his name is King Herod and where they can find him. A discussion is held in the king's court. Herod cunningly convinces the wise men that he would wish to pay homage to the new king himself and extracts as much information as possible. He dispatches the wise men to seek out the king and return to him with a full report. The king in discussion with his courtiers reveals that he will destroy this impostor as soon as he discovers his whereabouts from these 'wise fools'! Wise men meet children from Joseph's family who show them the way. Discussion with Joseph and Mary about the gifts that each has brought. One child looks downcast because she had only a little wooden flute to give Jesus. Joseph and the wise men discuss with the children that the greatest gift that any king would want was always a loving, loyal heart. Their gifts were as nothing compared with that. Wise men intercepted by the same stranger who spoke to the shepherds, who tells them of Herod's evil plan. So the wise men laugh at Herod calling them wise fools and outwit him at his own game, by leaving a false trail and going home another way.

Part 4 — 2 February: Candlemas

Again, the celebration could be in the school or in the church, but we have Mary and Joseph continuing the story as they take Jesus to the Temple and meet Simeon and Anna.

Suggestions for improvised or scripted scenes

Characters: Jesus, Mary and Joseph, Anna and Simeon, passers-by, people in the Temple, pigeon-seller.

Scenes: Mary wraps Jesus in a shawl and goes with Joseph to buy two young pigeons to make an offering in the Temple as they present their baby son to God. Discussion with the pigeon-seller about the cost of the birds. Joseph carries the offering as they enter the Temple. Simeon comes forward to greet Mary and Joseph and the child. Anna too comes forward to talk with Mary and Joseph about their child. Mary and Joseph leave the Temple after the ceremony. Mary is worried about what she has heard and shares this with Joseph. He reassures Mary that God will look after them.

You will notice that the Christmas event lasts for six weeks. In this way the children are living through the events and celebrating them to the full. So often when schools return after Christmas, within a week Christmas is forgotten. Epiphany and Candlemas are lucky if they even get a mention. To continue the celebration in the form of a serialized play helps the community to enter into the event. Frequently, we rush through the whole Christmas story from beginning to end before it has actually even begun in our parish life. If we compare the amount of time and preparation and the emphasis laid on secular preparations for Christmas with the time and preparation and emphasis for celebrating the feast as it should be, is it any wonder that the god of the market-place makes a greater impression on young minds than the God in whose name we celebrate this feast?

PREPARATION CHART FOR CHRISTMAS CELEBRATION

Class	In charge of preparing
Reception Teacher:	
Year 1 Teacher:	
Year 2 Teacher:	
Year 3 Teacher:	
Year 4 Teacher:	
Tear 5 Teacher:	
Year 6 Teacher:	
Parents	
Parish	

Celebrating Easter

The following suggestions are designed for maximum flexibility. They can be enacted and celebrated in the following ways:

1. Parish, home and school working together and based in the church and school.
2. Home and school working together and based in the school.
3. School working alone and based in the school only.

Just as at Christmas the community recognizes the need for a Christmas crib to help people enter into the feast, so too at Easter there is a need for a focal point. The construction of an Easter garden can not only serve to help the liturgy but also be an effective way of involving as many people as possible in its construction.

Ideally the following celebrations should be in the parish and begun on Easter Sunday and continued through Easter Monday.

Creating the right atmosphere

Banners and backdrops: prepare white and gold banners which can be hung in the school and the church to create a sense of festival and celebration.

It is important to use all the senses in creating the right backdrop and atmosphere to the big feasts. Easter is our greatest feast and deserves all the creativity and preparation that the parish and school can gather for its celebration. The Easter garden will help as a starting point to begin telling the story of the Easter events. The Easter garden can be either inside the church or outside in the grounds.

The celebration

The celebration begins with the telling of the story of Mary Magdalene and the women finding the tomb empty.

As with the Christmas improvised scenes and plays, don't be afraid to encourage small groups to create their own version of each story.

The story continues in the Upper Room with the women trying to convince the disciples that Jesus is risen. Included in this scene is the story of Thomas and his meeting with Jesus. The third scene takes us down the road to Emmaus. A school drive or parish path can be used as the setting for this. The meal at the end of the road to Emmaus can be celebrated by the whole parish and school sharing in a meal together and celebrating the fact that Jesus is with them.

Easter Monday

The whole parish is invited to a special barbecue to recall the post-resurrection appearances of Jesus that centred around a mealtime. Invite family groups/small groups to gather together around a very primitive barbecue to recall the type of fire that Jesus and his friends would have eaten around. Invite people to make as many different kinds of bread as they can to share with the parish for the meal. Have the bread collected in one central place and placed in wicker baskets, one basket for each group. Invite the people to bring fish that can be cooked on an open fire of this kind. Select one person from each group to be the story-teller who will recall and tell the stories of Jesus sharing a meal with his friends by the seashore.

PREPARATION CHART FOR EASTER CELEBRATION

Class	In charge of preparing
Reception Teacher:	
Year 1 Teacher:	
Year 2 Teacher:	
Year 3 Teacher:	
Year 4 Teacher:	
Tear 5 Teacher:	
Year 6 Teacher:	
Parents	
Parish	

Celebrating Pentecost

In the school's preparation for Pentecost there will be a lot of focus on diversity and unity. The school would have looked at all the wonderful cultures represented in its community and how they are all part of God's family. This is what we will be celebrating in our whole-school/ parish/home celebration.

The following is a suggestion for celebrating within the school premises but also remembering to invite friends from the parish and families.

Environment

We used a strong focal point for Christmas and Easter; it is very important that we do the same at Pentecost. The use of strong symbols such as fire, wind, water, the dove, red, all help to enter into the mood of the celebration. It would be most appropriate to display a simplified but very large map of the world on a prominent wall as a backdrop to the celebration. Mark on our map all the places where the children and the friends of the school come from. Also displayed in the area where the celebration is to take place can be samples of food from the different countries where our children, their parents or grandparents were born. The idea is to create a school atmosphere where no one nationality dominates but the richness and gift of each can be displayed.

Nursery and infants

Nursery and infant children can be dressed in costumes representing the different countries that make up our community. They can also be given streamers to wave made from silver and red tin foil to depict wind and fire.

Each class can choose a different aspect of the celebration to depict in its own way.

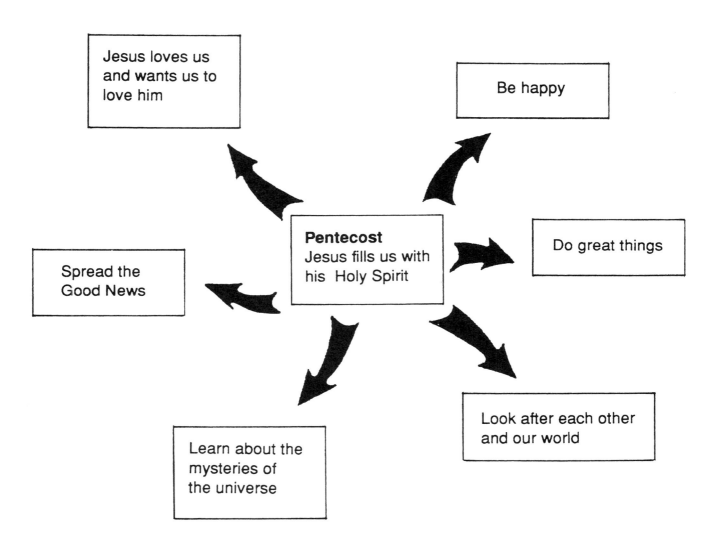

Celebrating our gifts

All the children are invited to display something that they are good at. This could be as simple as a drawing or a piece of writing, or as elaborate as a recital, dance, judo demonstration, football skills, wearing a uniform of Beavers, Cubs or Scouts, Rainbows, Brownies or Guides. The school gathers for a day of celebration where each child or group of children shares its gifts and talents. It is important that every child and member of staff contributes in some form to make the point that we have all been given gifts and they are for sharing and to make one another happy.

The celebration can end with the sharing of the foods from the different countries.

PREPARATION CHART FOR PENTECOST CELEBRATION

Class	In charge of preparing
Reception Teacher:	
Year 1 Teacher:	
Year 2 Teacher:	
Year 3 Teacher:	
Year 4 Teacher:	
Tear 5 Teacher:	
Year 6 Teacher:	
Parents	
Parish	

Sending forth — goodbye

Just as the Welcome theme is very important for the whole life of the school, so too is the final theme, Sending forth — Goodbye.

This final theme includes a missioning celebration which not only involves those in your school community, but also, it is hoped, representatives from the new schools that your pupils are now moving to. They come to receive your pupils in the name of the secondary school and form an important link between the two communities.

It is very important to help the children overcome their fear of moving on to the next stage whether it be junior to secondary, infants to juniors or nursery to infants. Every change to a new stage, new classroom and teacher is a big step. Because of the importance of each of these steps in the journey of the child through the school it is good to celebrate and ritualize the event and allow all those involved to prepare to say 'goodbye'. It is also important to recall the past time together, to affirm and to thank, as well as to say sorry. As with the Welcome theme, the whole school needs to be involved in saying goodbye and sending their friends on to the next stage of the journey.

In their classroom work each age group will be looking in depth at this theme. The following are suggestions for celebrating this event.

In this celebration the community is: Saying goodbye, Remembering, Anointing, Missioning.

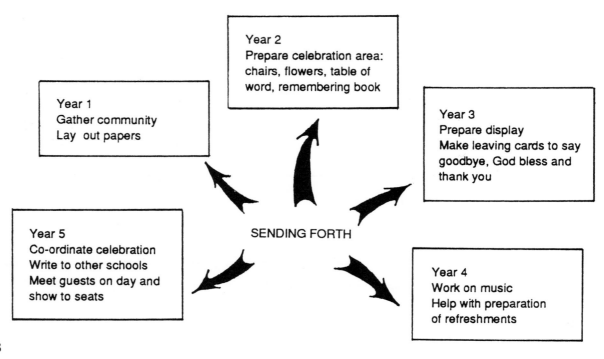

Year 1
Gather community
Lay out papers

Year 2
Prepare celebration area:
chairs, flowers, table of
word, remembering book

Year 3
Prepare display
Make leaving cards to say
goodbye, God bless and
thank you

SENDING FORTH

Year 5
Co-ordinate celebration
Write to other schools
Meet guests on day and
show to seats

Year 4
Work on music
Help with preparation
of refreshments

Saying goodbye

We all have memories of 'last days'. Some were pretty heartless, leaving us with a feeling that maybe folk were really rather glad to see the back of us, or simply as the last day drew near we realized that those remaining were more concerned with the new people coming in than with us going out. Most of us would like to think that would never happen in our school but sometimes the hurly-burly of the end of term actually leaves some people, staff and pupils alike, wondering just how much people really do care.

Obviously, the preparations for new people coming in are essential. But the way in which they are carried out can be a very positive experience for everyone even for those who are not going to be there in the new term.

Saying goodbye in a way that says 'we care about you', 'we love you and will miss you' gives courage and affirmation to the person leaving the community. It also allows those who remain the opportunity to express their feelings about the person leaving. This is expressed by presenting a goodbye card to each person who is leaving.

Layout of celebration

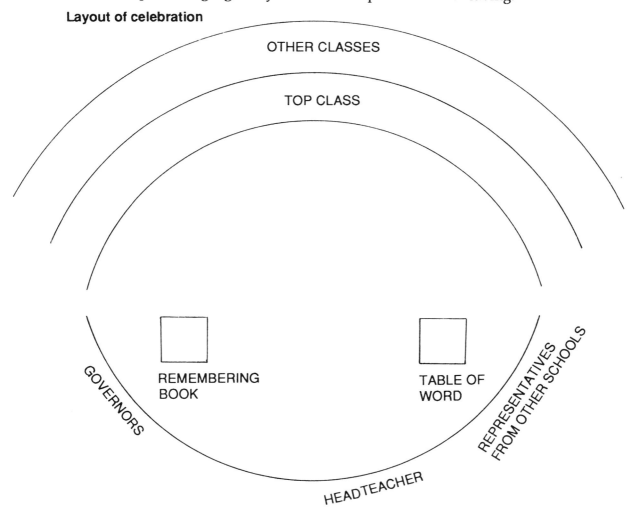

Remembering

As we say goodbye we are also saying that we will *remember you*. Not just superficially, but by each person signing their name in the *Remembering Book* beside their picture. This book is given a special place in the school and the names in it are recalled at appropriate occasions. It is important to explain again to the community that *remembering* is something that *Jesus* told us to do. In remembering people they are made present in a special way. Something of that person always stays with us. We are all affected and changed by the people we share our lives with. We remember and we thank each person for what he or she has been for the community.

Anointing

(Oil of gladness can be simply made using any scented body oil.)

To anoint someone is to honour them, to show that they are someone special. In this celebration the headteacher, who is the leader of this Catholic community, calls each person who is leaving by name and invites them to step forward. They are then anointed by the head-teacher with the *oil of gladness*, not only as a sign of how much we honour them but as a sign of our joy and gladness at having known them and all that they are for us. Anointing is also a sign of con-secration, of being specially chosen by God to become his instrument. Priests, prophets and kings were all anointed and consecrated to God and became sharers in the spirit of God (1 Samuel 16:13).

Missioning

Having anointed the people who are leaving, the community now sends them forth to their new community. If it has been possible to contact the new schools that your pupils are going on to and invite representatives from those schools to be present at this final celebration, they are now called forward to receive the new members of their community. In the name of the senior schools that they represent, they thank the primary school for preparing them for this day and welcome them to their new school. If appropriate, the top class pupils and the representatives of the new schools then leave the celebration together.

School links

Both the Welcome and the Goodbye celebrations are excellent opportunities for strengthening the links between the different levels in the Catholic school system. It is important that infant and primary schools as well as primary and secondary schools are in close liaison over these very important occasions in the pupils' lives. Thus we reinforce the idea that we are one community, different sections but all equally concerned for its members at all stages.

PREPARATION CHART FOR SENDING FORTH CELEBRATION

Class	In charge of preparing
Reception Teacher:	
Year 1 Teacher:	
Year 2 Teacher:	
Year 3 Teacher:	
Year 4 Teacher:	
Tear 5 Teacher:	
Year 6 Teacher:	
Parents	
Parish	

Part 3

THE RE CURRICULUM

Introducing the RE curriculum

The school eucharist and the whole-school celebrations are of course an aspect of religious education: they are presented here as part of a context of religious education in the classroom, and this in turn should permeate the whole curriculum.

The plan below should make clearer the relationship between the whole-school celebration and the work of the classroom.

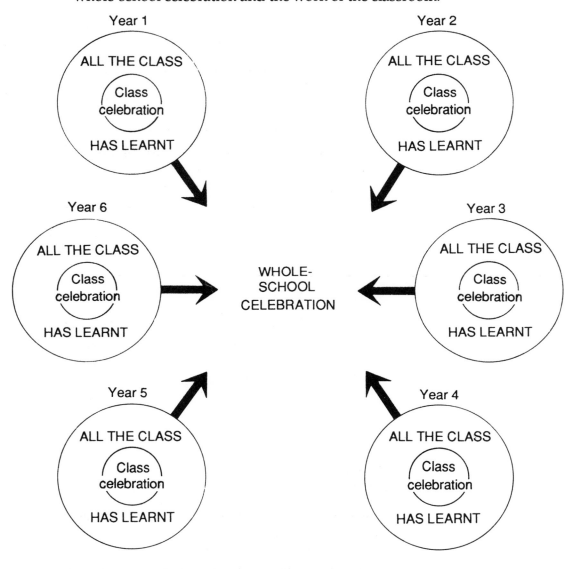

Each whole-school celebration draws on the classwork of every class: this classwork is guided by the syllabus for that class, and the syllabus follows on pages 77-82.

You will see that the syllabus is divided into three sections: teaching, worship and values. The work in the left-hand column (teaching) is closely linked with the whole curriculum of that class. Much of the material in this syllabus is cross-curricular, and may therefore be studied in the time allocated to other curriculum areas.

An example:

RE Syllabus	National Curriculum Science
In Year 1 pupils look at the differences between them in shape and size and give thanks for their variety.	Level 1: pupils should know that there is a wide variety of living things which includes human beings.
In Year 2, in the Thanksgiving theme, pupils study how plants and humans grow.	Level 2: pupils should know that plants and animals need certain conditions to sustain life; understand how living things are looked after.

By studying RE and Science together they are made aware of the wonder and actuality of God's creation.

But this is taken further. The second column of the syllabus (worship) gives themes for celebration, and the class does not leave what it has learnt in Science or RE simply as knowledge. RE time is spent in class celebrations of each theme, as well as whole-school celebrations.

What to teach

Choosing materials for RE should be guided by reflection on what children should experience, know and understand at the various ages.

At any given level from Years 1 to 6 you must be aware of:
- what is being taught at that level
- how it is expressed and celebrated
- what are the implications for life in the world today.

These three roots run through the whole of the Church's life and teaching as expressed in the liturgical cycle.

The themes

We have selected the main highlights of the Church's year and the school year and used these as our framework. They are:

Welcome
Giving thanks
All Souls and All Saints
Advent
Christmas
Epiphany
Candlemas
Lent
Easter
Pentecost
Saints
Sending forth — goodbye

You will see these twelve themes occurring each year for Years 1 to 6.

The syllabus presented here is only an outline to enable headteachers to get an overview of what is taught throughout the school. Detailed plans of what is taught in every classroom on every theme throughout the year will follow in the Teacher's Book and the pupils' books. This will provide a complete primary RE course, *The Rainbow People*.

On pages 85 and 86 some examples are given of the way in which what is studied in RE also covers other parts of the curriculum; teachers will be able to work out more for themselves when they look in detail at what is taught in any one theme at any one level. An example of this is presented on page 88.

Integrating the reception class

Year 1 material for both teachers and children has been produced with maximum flexibility to enable both the reception teacher and Year 1 teacher to select according to the wider age range at this level. Careful record-keeping will ensure that children do not repeat material unnecessarily.

The Outline Syllabus: Year 1 (5–6 years) and Reception (4-5 years)

THEME	TEACHING	WORSHIP	VALUES
Welcome	Learning about God's family and belonging. Learning about our new family.	Celebrating each special person.	Each person is unique, valued, to be respected. Gift to the family.
Giving thanks	Gifts God gives. My body: differences. My family.	Thanking God for our bodies and gifts. Sharing.	All are good.
All Souls and All Saints	All part of *one family*, past, present and future. Everyone in God's care and love.	Celebrating people of *all ages* known to children.	Remembering special people that we know or have known.
Advent	Purple — waiting time. Remembering Jesus' birthday. Getting ready. Babies. New life. Who is Jesus?	Getting ready for special events. 'Preparing' experiences. Special visitors. Jesus' birthday preparations.	Care and attention. Things of importance needing special care.
Christmas	White time. A very special baby: Jesus, given to us as our friend. Christmas is Jesus' birthday.	Welcoming Jesus into our home and school. Telling Jesus how happy we are he's here.	Christmas is about a special family, people and families. Importance of people and families.
Epiphany	Jesus' friends come to see him, bring presents, etc.	Making and giving gift for someone I love. Gift as symbol.	Showing we love others by visiting them.
Candlemas	Mary and Joseph say 'Thank you' to God for Jesus.	Candles, light. Birthday cake has candles.	Gratitude, saying thank you.
Lent	Purple — sorry time. Putting things right, making up and showing people how to do things as Jesus did.	Loving each other by saying sorry. Telling Jesus that we want to be friends because he loves us and them.	Forgiveness.
Easter	White time. Easter garden. Telling story, new life all over the world.	Celebrating new life. Babies, animals, flowers, etc. New day.	Good things always happen even when we think they won't.
Pentecost	Red time. Gifts, new life, each other, special things we can do.	Celebrate sharing our gifts with one another. Talent sharing.	Giftedness of each person. Learning to give of yourself. Affirmation of gifts and self-worth.
Saints and feasts	Special school saint or person school is called after (feast).	Celebrating life story of feast or saint. Saying thank you for that person.	Related to saint and what he or she stood for. Building up idea that we are all called to be special.
Sending forth 'Goodbye'	Moving up, a year older, grown. Recall the year: how much have they discovered about their life in God's world? Likes/dislikes. Going to make a new beginning.	Saying goodbye to school year, class, teacher, friends. Thanking God for each other.	Responsibility for what has been discovered and learnt.

The Outline Syllabus: Year 2 (6–7 years)

THEME	TEACHING	WORSHIP	VALUES
Welcome	Prepare to welcome new friends into our community. Family of God. Names are important.	Telling our part of the story of our community.	Each person is unique. People bring joy and happiness to one another.
Giving thanks	Food for our bodies. Food for our hearts (love for each other). Growing plants which can be eaten, watching them grow.	Saying thank you for the gifts of the earth and each other. Celebrations with water.	Taking care of and respecting things that grow.
All Souls and All Saints	Remembering people we know who have died. Talking about death, feelings about death, moving to a new life after death.	Special book, pictures of people we want to remember. Those who have died. Remembering in church.	Learning from people who have gone before us.
Advent	Time to get ready. Symbols: Advent wreath, cards, prayers, badges, Mary candle, recall purple.	Celebrations with Advent wreath and Mary candle.	Putting Jesus first.
Christmas	The people in the Christmas story: Holy Family, shepherds, kings, angels, innkeeper, wise men. Telling each one's story.	Putting themselves into the Christmas story. I am the Good Shepherd.	Power of Christmas, bringing people together, happy time.
Epiphany	Gifts, symbolism, wise men coming from afar. Jesus has given us so many gifts — which three do we treasure the most?	We are gifts to each other. Thanking God for these gifts.	Respecting each other.
Candlemas	Story of the presentation.	Light.	Hope. Jesus is always with us.
Lent	Lent is the springtime of the church. A time for planting and preparing, of working hard. Garden, park, farm imagery.	Jesus' choices. Being strong in mind, heart, body and soul. It takes strength to say sorry, to make difficult choices.	Development of conscience, good/bad. Link with life. Making ourselves strong in mind and body to do our very best.
Easter	The people in the Easter Sunday stories.	Celebrating joy and happiness because our greatest friend loves us.	Overcoming hurt with love.
Pentecost	The people in the story. Holy Spirit.	Using symbols of the Holy Spirit: fire, water, wind.	Holy Spirit gives us strength because it is Jesus' love burning in us.
Saints and feasts	St Peter and St Paul — telling their stories.	Celebrating second chances so that we can go on to show the world how great Jesus is.	The power forgiveness has to set people free.
Sending forth 'Goodbye'	We are chosen, given lots of gifts and knowledge, now we must move on. Looking at what we are called to do. Recall Peter and Paul.	Remembering special moments this year when Jesus has really spoken to us through each other. Saying thank you.	Recognizing Jesus as our friend through the goodness of others.

The Outline Syllabus: Year 3 (7–8 years)

THEME	TEACHING	WORSHIP	VALUES
Welcome	Prepare practical welcome of new friends into building. Baptism and the significance of names and the name of the school.	Telling our part of the story. Celebrating names.	Taking responsibility for new friends. Importance of names. God knowing us all by name.
Giving thanks	The creation story.	Celebrating creation.	Taking care of our planet.
All Souls and All Saints	Selected outstanding people who have gone before us. Their lives and example. Different cultures.	Celebrating those who care for us and other and the challenge of continuing their work.	Our responsibility in continuing to build up the Body of Christ, the family of God.
Advent	The Jesse Tree to tell the story of where Jesus came from. We remember: Noah, Abraham, Moses, David, who all prepared for Jesus' coming.	Remembering great people in our families who have prepared the way for us. The qualities we share with them.	Importance of our ancestors and fathers and mothers of the faith.
Christmas	Christmas celebrated around the world. Rich/poor divide. Different cultures and their traditions.	Finding ways of celebrating without spending a lot of money — celebrating with people.	Christmas joy found in *people*, not things.
Epiphany	Gifts we can give to others in greater need. Giving without counting the cost. Class project for people in need.	Bringing a ray of light and hope to people in need.	Responsibility.
Candlemas	Jesus' coming into the world as a ray of hope. How are we hope for others?	Lighting a candle for someone who needs us. Symbolism.	Hope in our lives.
Lent	Link with giving thanks. Creation. Explore the environment issue.	Celebrating life on earth and our responsibility for it.	Care for all forms of life.
Easter	The story that Jesus is risen spreads. Emmaus story. Jesus cooking breakfast. Beginning of early Christian community. People gather together. So great is God's love for us that he raised Jesus from the dead.	Meals as times when Jesus is specially with us.	Evil has been overcome.
Pentecost	Early community begins. Church is formed. Holy Spirit fires hearts of those who hear the Word.	Telling people that Jesus is risen and alive.	Speaking good words.
Saints and feasts	St Francis of Assisi. Love of creation and poor.	Continuing the work of St Francis. Prayers, songs of joy about creation.	Depending on life of saints chosen.
Sending forth 'Goodbye'	As the early Christians discovered the 'Good News' they went out to tell others. How can we do this?	Celebrating 'Good News'.	Being 'Good News'.

The Outline Syllabus: Year 4 (8–9 years)

THEME	TEACHING	WORSHIP	VALUES
Welcome	Telling the story of the community. Newcomers and people with other languages.	Celebration of welcome. As we belong to a community we all have an effect on one another.	Imagining how others feel. Making people feel at home.
Giving thanks	Thanking God for our family, our community, our church.	Celebrating our unity.	Harmony, unity.
All Souls and All Saints	The early Church and the Church today. Paul's travels and letters.	Celebrating great people. Recognizing God working through us.	'Building up' not 'pulling down'.
Advent	Mary, our Mother, Mother of Jesus, Mother of the Church. Mary getting ready for the baby. Mothers and babies.	Celebrating women and mothers. Using the Mary candle. The Rosary.	Respect for women, and other cultures.
Christmas	Mary and her child Jesus as portrayed through art around the world and seen through different cultures. Collecting cards and artistic impressions.	Celebrating the giving of new life — animals and children. Symbols of life.	Using the art work, select attributes: compassionate, tender, loving, etc.
Epiphany	Looking at the three wise men through art, what images, symbolism.	Different styles of giving thanks and praise. Pomp and ceremony. Simple. Compare wise men with shepherds.	All are acceptable to Jesus. It's the heart, the intention, that counts.
Candlemas	Mothers saying thank you for children. Simeon and Anna.	Celebrations with mothers.	Valuing children.
Lent	Jesus as Saviour. Situations at home (UK) where the family of God is broken. Lack of food, homes. Children suffering. Lent theme of justice from OT.	Celebrating overcoming suffering. Healing. Stories of healing in NT.	God does not want his children to suffer.
Easter	New life begins. The women hear the good news first. Mary Magdalene. Women in OT and NT. How they stayed faithful.	Celebrating with bread. Making bread. Symbolism. Baking. 'I am the bread of life.' Sharing meals with bread of different kinds.	Called to be one people in community. Sharing our bread.
Pentecost	A new community comes together. Features of that: caring for one another, sharing everything, proclaiming.	Faithful to the breaking of bread.	Courage to believe.
Saints and feasts	Saints from the East (link with Epiphany). Giving life for Jesus. Missionaries going out to preach.	Celebrating the Eastern Church, its people and its gifts.	All races and cultures are equal.
Sending forth 'Goodbye'	Looking at where the class has come from and where they are being sent to — next class — in the future. Moving into unknown. Link with missionaries and how they had to make a leap of faith.	Believing in God's goodness that 'all will be well'.	Trust in God and trust in ourselves.

The Outline Syllabus: Year 5 (9–10 years)

THEME	TEACHING	WORSHIP	VALUES
Welcome	The history of the school as a Christian community and links with the early Church.	Celebrating new friends.	Sharing our lives, our time, ourselves. Finding our way in treasure trail. Light.
Giving thanks	People who have brought Christianity to our country.	Thanking God for the gift of the Good News.	Courage to say what you know to be true. Standing up for your faith.
All Souls and All Saints	People in our lives who have taught us our faith. Remembering them. Link with Giving thanks.	Celebrating the gifts of faith and knowledge.	Recognizing that God works through us.
Advent	Prophets who prepared the way and continue today. Change.	Celebrating courage. Standing up to injustice. St Nicholas.	Justice.
Christmas	Jesus brings peace for all. Christmas among the poor at home and abroad. Justice.	The Christmas story as seen through the eyes of those who have few or no possessions.	Jesus loved the poor, the lowly, the simple, children.
Epiphany	Contrast wise men's gifts with the shepherds' presence. Presence and presents.	Celebrating *being* a friend to someone with nothing to give except ourselves.	Valuing people enough not to need presents to prove it.
Candlemas	A light shines in the night. Being a light in the lives of the poor.	Lights for justice. Flames burning. Amnesty, etc.	Jesus is the Light of the World.
Lent	Jesus lived and gave his life to show us how to love one another. Follow themes through NT showing Jesus' attitudes towards those most in need.	Celebrations of forgiveness. Bring people together as Jesus did. Loss of Alleluia.	Forgiveness.
Easter	The Easter services telling the story. Triduum.	Easter through music. Return of Alleluia.	Joy.
Pentecost	Gifts of the Holy Spirit and ways in which we use them as God's chosen children. Confirmation.	Celebrating our giftedness with the whole community.	Recognizing that all have gifts.
Saints and feasts	Corpus Christi.	Develop whole-school celebration.	We are *all* responsible for the community. The strength is measured by the weakest link.
Sending forth 'Goodbye'	Remember Giving thanks and All Souls and All Saints. Now our turn. Prepare to celebrate with whole school to send out friends in Year 6.	Celebration of mission. Taking up senior place in school.	Responsibility. Each has a job to do.

The Outline Syllabus: Year 6 (10–11 years)

THEME	TEACHING	WORSHIP	VALUES
Welcome	Leadership in the (Christian) community. Concern for past and future of members of the community. Knowing who we are.	Celebrating the past and the future. Called to be disciples. Handing on responsibility.	Knowing who we are, telling our story. Responsibility for others.
Giving thanks	How the Jews celebrated the 'harvest'. Other faiths and Christian Churches and ways in which they celebrate giving thanks.	Celebrating together with other Christians, other faiths.	There are many ways to God.
All Souls and All Saints	Looking at life after death. Talking about images of God. Heaven, Hell. Looking at Halloween. St Michael.	Celebrating with our brothers and sisters in the after-life, 'Communion of Saints'. Saints' Day Parade.	Link between life on earth and life after death. We choose what kind of life, good or bad.
Advent	Relating Advent themes to life of school community with emphasis on the school environment. Isaiah, Advent Antiphons, John the Baptist.	Celebrating light. Light in other faiths. Mary Mother of Peace.	Taking seriously our responsibility for responding to the Church's year.
Christmas	The Christmas story in modern time. Jesus born today? Bringer of peace. Bible accounts.	Celebrating Jesus being 'born again' in our time. Celebrating peace.	Understanding that the Christmas event is for all time.
Epiphany	The wise men and Herod. What is the meaning of this/the story in today's time? Choices. Seeing the truth. Wisdom.	Celebrating God's care of us — as with wise men and Holy Family.	Wisdom — not easily flattened. Being alert.
Candlemas	Simeon's prayer. Meaning. Where can we see God working in our lives, in the world?	Celebrations of light.	God is always at work through us.
Lent	The story of Holy Week, time of Jesus. Palm Sunday. Holy Saturday. The struggle between good and evil.	Seeing parallels today. Entering into them.	Understanding sacrifice and suffering.
Easter	Thomas — and people who found it difficult to believe that Jesus was alive. Doubt and uncertainty. Gift of faith.	Understanding that we sometimes doubt. Learning to trust. Leaps of faith.	Learning to trust.
Pentecost	The Holy Spirit. What do we mean — working in our lives? Trinity.	Trinitarian celebrations based on love.	Love — the greatest power in heaven and on earth.
Saints and feasts	Ascension — Jesus returns to Father. Moving on as the class will. Life as journey.	Celebrating the excitement of moving on.	Learning to 'let go'.
Sending forth 'Goodbye'	Being 'missioned', 'anointed', 'sent out'. Looking at Scripture for examples (in Gospels and Acts; OT for anointing)	Celebration with whole school.	Our community gives us a challenge. We are responsible for it.

Progression

As children go up the school they require more challenging and difficult work in each year. Thus, in the syllabus, the same theme is approached in each year *not only* with different content, *but also* with activities and learning goals suitable for the age group concerned.

The linkage with the National Curriculum, which has been based on the development of the child, helps to ensure that this is the case.

One example of progression within a theme is shown in the table below and again in the earlier elaboration of Welcome on pages 44-53.

Theme: Welcome		
Year	Level of difficulty of task	Degree of responsibility and understanding
1	Learning new names, rooms in school, items in classroom.	Simple concern for each other. All part of God's family.
2	Planning and carrying out simple practical task (hats, badges). Planning and carrying out simple social task.	Responsibility for helping one other class — Year 1. Imagining feelings of new people. Wanting to show our love.
3	Research on meaning of names. Research and presenting findings and proposing improvements in school building.	All God's children in school. Understanding of multi-cultural background of people in school. Responsibility for all users of school building — area of concern has widened.
4	Treasure trail: a far more complicated task to plan and carry out in terms of technology, geography.	Responsibility for whole-school celebration: concern for whole school and its well-being.
5	Research on school and its history as a Christian community and presenting findings to whole school. Linking this with the early Church. Understanding similarities and differences.	Concern widens to include whole parish and whole Church. Concern to pass this on.
6	Writing letters to new people they have never met and following up in person. Making a book to record the history of past members of the school.	Assuming almost adult responsibility for directly greeting and guiding newcomers (adult and child). Concern for those who have gone before into the wider community and passing on this information in a book, i.e. for past and future.

Record sheet

The syllabus is structured to enable you to check easily on the following:
- what is being taught
- how this is developmental
- what each child has experienced, come to know and understood.

This can easily be checked using the Pupil Record Sheet on page 96.

Links with the National Curriculum

The National Curriculum aims to promote 'the spiritual, moral, cultural, mental and physical development of pupils . . . and prepare such pupils for the opportunities, responsibilities and experiences of adult life' (Education Reform Act, 1988) and to do this through a developmental process. Therefore, by linking the National Curriculum with this RE syllabus, which is based on the liturgical cycle of the Church's year, we are in fact linking two processes that are complementary.

In the United States, Canada, Scotland and Ireland the National Curriculum does not apply, but since children's development follows the same pattern, the work we have linked to the RE curriculum is likely to be suitable and will in most cases be what the teachers are doing with the children.

Pages 85 and 86 show some examples of the correspondence between the National Curriculum subjects and the RE syllabus. Models I and II are suggested aids to planning the curriculum.

KEY STAGE 1

Subject	Topic	RE Syllabus
English: Speaking and listening	Speaking and listening in group activities, including imaginative investigations; listening attentively and responding to stories and poems. Talk with the teacher. Give simple instructions. Ask questions.	All themes
Reading		All themes
Writing	Use pictures, symbols and isolated letters to communicate meaning. Writing sentences.	All themes
Spelling	Understand the difference between drawing and writing, numbers and letters.	All themes
Science	Pupils should be finding out about themselves. Developing ideas about how they grow.	Giving thanks Y2
	Should be introduced to ideas about how to keep healthy.	Thanking God for our lives Y1
	Should consider similarities and differences between themselves and other children.	Giving thanks Y1
Mathematics	Shape and space. My place in the classroom.	Welcome Y1
	Handling data. Route around the school.	Welcome Y2
Technology	Pupils should — be taught that a system is made of related parts, e.g. school — identify the jobs done by parts of the system (kitchen, hall, etc.) — give a sequence of instructions to produce a desired result — route round class or school — realize that materials and equipment need to be safely stored and maintained — container for storing pencils safely	All of these are to be found in the Welcome theme.
History	Pupils should — be helped to develop an awareness of the past through stories about historical events — have opportunities to listen to adults talking about their past — be exposed to written sources — become familiar with different types of buildings — be taught about saints — be taught about religious festivals	Welcome Bible School, church Welcome — patron saint of school Feasts and festivals of the liturgical year
Geography	Pupils should be able to — follow directions round a classroom, school and site — observe and talk about home and school — follow a route using a plan — identify activities carried out by parents and people who work in the school — talk about the uses of homes, schools and places of worship — talk about the people they have seen working and what they do	Welcome covers all these topics.

Subject	Topic	RE Syllabus
English: Speaking and listening	Relate real or imaginary events in a connected narrative, which conveys meaning to a group of pupils, the teacher or another known adult. Convey a simple message. Listen, ask and respond to questions and comment on what has been said. Give, receive and follow instructions. Participate in a presentation.	All themes
Reading	Read aloud and silently. Listen attentively to stories, talk about setting, story line and characters and recall significant details. Use reference books to find out more information. Develop their own views and support them in discussion.	
Writing	The writing and telling of stories. Paying attention to meaning; deeper meanings and clarity.	All themes at the appropriate level
Science	Pupils should — know basic life processes — know that air is all around us — be able to explain the water cycle — know that human activity may produce local changes in the earth's surface, air and water — that some waste materials can be recycled — be able to describe the sources, implications and possible prevention of pollution — be able to describe the main stages in the human life cycle	Thanking God for creation Y3 Taking care of your planet Y3 All Souls and All Saints Y6
Technology	Pupils should recognise the aesthetic qualities of natural and manufactured materials.	Thanking God for creation Y3
History	Pupils should be able to — use words and phrases relating to the passing of time, e.g. BC, AD — make connections between events and situations in different periods of history — investigate differences between versions of past events	Advent Y3, Y5 Advent Y3, Y5; All Souls Y4, Y5 Christmas Y4, Y6
Geography	Pupils should — learn to identify on globes and maps places they are studying — investigate features of other localities and how these features might affect people's lives	All Souls Y3 Christmas Y4, Y6

Model I

Curriculum Planning Sheet

Year: I
Term: September to Christmas

RE Theme	English	Maths	Science	Technology	History	Geography	Music	PE	Art
Welcome	Participate in group discussion. Recognise written words.	Shape and space. My place in the classroom.	/	School – a system of related parts. Jobs done by parts e.g. kitchen. Storing materials.	Ideas about past of their school.	Follow directions round school.	Simple songs.	Describe what they and others are doing.	Drawing. Colouring.
Giving thanks	Use pictures to communicate meaning.	/	Parts of the body, how to keep healthy. Similarities and differences between children.	/	/	Names of countries that children's families are from.	Simple songs.	/	Drawing, Colouring.
All Souls and All Saints	/	/	Bigger and smaller children, older and younger.	/	Understand older and younger	/	Simple songs.	Learning to play with others. Sharing equipment.	/
Advent	Listen to a story. Talk about story.	/	Where babies come from.	Discuss what is needed in an imaginary situation; baby expected.	Story from the past.	/	Simple songs.	/	Making Cards.

Model II: short-term planning

Example of planning sheet for each theme

<table>
<tr><td colspan="2" align="center">PLANNING SHEET</td></tr>
<tr><td colspan="2">Theme: Giving thanks
Year: 2</td></tr>
<tr><td align="center">Religious Education</td><td align="center">Relation to rest of curriculum</td></tr>
<tr>
<td>Project
Growing things in the classroom and learning about conditions needed for growth
— water
— sunlight
— earth</td>
<td>Make and record observations (Science 1, level 2)
Know there is a wide variety of living things, including human beings
Know that plants and animals need certain conditions to sustain life (Science 2, level 1)</td>
</tr>
<tr>
<td>Discussion
What we need to grow
— food?
— water?
— laughter?
— friends?</td>
<td>Take part in group discussion (Oral English, levels 1 and 2)
Know that the basic life processes are common to human beings and the other living things they have studied (Science 3, level 3)</td>
</tr>
<tr>
<td>Celebration
— water and blessing
— water and baptism; babies
— earth is blessed by rain
— sprinkling at Sunday Mass</td>
<td>Sing a variety of simple songs (Music 1, level 1)
Use movement to show moods and feelings (PE, level 1)</td>
</tr>
</table>

Sacraments flowcharts

The following sacrament flowcharts illustrate where the specific teaching about the sacraments, Baptism, Reconciliation, Eucharist and Confirmation, can be identified throughout the syllabus. The pupils will be introduced to all seven sacraments but a more detailed study of the remaining three will appear at secondary level.

Baptism flowchart

Reception and Year 1
Hear that their parents took them to the church to be baptized
See a water font and water being blessed
Experience being blessed with water
Experience receiving new garments; great joy
See a white garment for a baby at baptism
Children of other faiths: how initiated
Can be blessed and given new garments

Year 2
Remember their own welcome
Hear again the story of their baptism
How they were sprinkled and blessed, learnt to
make sign of cross, trinitarian words
Symbolism of water. Telling the story of Jesus' baptism

Year 3
Building on Years 1 and 2
Names: given a special name: God knows us by name

Year 4
Making people feel at home, belonging to a community
What happens to you happens to me

Year 5
Light, the candle — finding your way
Experience: helping others to find their way,
to learn the lifestyle of the school,
explaining what will be expected of them

Year 6
Anointing
Will have experienced many groups of children
being anointed and sent out
Links will be made between anointing and baptism and
the biblical references to anointing of God's chosen people;
people set apart for a special task — anointing of David

Reconciliation flowchart

Reception and Year 1
Sorry time
Experience: Saying sorry is good and happy
Know: Jesus forgave people by loving them
Colour purple for Lent
Aware they need to say sorry
Naturalness

Year 2
Choosing and decision-making and their implications
Prayers of sorrow
Ways in which we say sorry — hugs, kisses, presents, words, kindness
Difficult to choose — making right decision makes things better —
saying sorry makes things better
Experience: reflecting on their life and what needs to change
Know: Jesus had to choose (certain friends); Zacchaeus

Year 3
Reconciliation — comfort, healing, helping people to love each other
Speaking, *words* and their power, act of contrition,
penance = doing something good after saying sorry
Beginning of idea of responsibility for other people and the world

Year 4
Choices we make affect wider circle of people
Conscience and the world, effects of sin, damage
Jesus chose tax collectors, etc. that others didn't like

Year 5
Feet washing
Following Jesus' footsteps — walk as he did
How Jesus treated sinners, people who hurt him
Rules, things we must do and things we must not do
Not judging people by outward appearance
Difficult to forgive
Forgiveness brings life — Peter, James, John, Andrew
Want to forgive as much as Jesus wanted to

Year 6
Struggle between good and evil — great battle in our lives and the world
Learning to trust
Environment
They are forgiven
Jesus forgave betrayers

Eucharist flowchart

Reception and Year 1 Gathering/Welcome
Being brought into a worshipping community
Belonging to this community
The joy of coming together. Celebrating and being happy together
All God's gifts are good and to be shared
Preparing for special occasions
We are Jesus' friends and we go to see him; he comes to see us
Say thank you for his friendship
Celebrating gifts

Year 2 The Word
Learning that the Bible is a very special book; looking after it;
carrying it in liturgical processions
God speaks through us and our story
God speaks through his special story in scripture
Remembering great people from the past
who have a special place in our story
Learning the story of each of the great seasons of the liturgical cycle
Speaking to one another, to God, and God to us

Year 3 Offertory
Learning that we are gifts
Importance of knowing names
Meaning of names
God has a special name for each one of us
Gifts of the earth: bread and wine. Making bread and wine
People who have prepared the way for us, and made
sacrifices so that we could benefit, given themselves
Giving of ourselves rather than buying presents
Early Christian community shared everything, especially bread and wine

Year 4 Reconciliation
Learning to understand we are all part of one body —
what happens to one happens to all
Harmony and unity
Called to build up not pull down
Learning to respect all people, especially women and children
Learning that Jesus loves us as we are, not because
we have a lot of possessions or are very clever
Being people who bring light and hope where there is division and sadness
Jesus brings hope where his family is broken and sad
Learning to comfort, heal, help, love in order to build up
Because of Jesus' love for us, evil has been overcome

Year 5 Jesus shares his life with us: Communion
Giving of themselves, their time, their love, their gifts
Recognizing that God wants all people to gather round his table:
eucharistic feast
Jesus' sacrifice when he stood up to injustice
against the poor and the weak
Jesus' reaching out the hand of friendship even to his enemies
Food strengthens, gives us courage
Eucharist source of unity with one another,
our God and giving us courage
Our responsibility for all members of the community,
especially the disadvantaged
Special prayers of the Eucharist: eucharistic prayer

Year 6   Thanksgiving
Looking back over the past and giving thanks for all
that we have learnt, shared and received
Learning to share the 'harvest' with everyone,
Christians and other faiths alike
Valuing our special faith and giving thanks for that
Remembering the communion of saints, those known to us
and those not known; the people who have gone before us
Thanking God for his care for us, as he cared for his Son
Wise Men and Holy Family
Thanking God with Simeon
Thanking God for the great sacrifice of his Son
Thanking God for the gift of faith
Thanksgiving for Father, Son and Holy Spirit
Thanking God for the gift of the community that
has supported us for the last six years

Confirmation flowchart

Irrespective of the age at which young people are confirmed these themes can be built on. Pentecost themes are the foundation.

Reception and Year 1
Fire, wind and water
Gifts
New life
Each other
The Pentecost story
Jesus' special friends grew in number each day

Year 2
Special people in the Pentecost story:
how did the Holy Spirit affect them? What did it make them do?
Special emphasis on the Holy Spirit giving strength

Year 3
The Holy Spirit giving courage to believe: what are the features
of a Christian, and of a Christian community?

Year 4
Speaking the good news
How the Church was formed out of the new community
Understand that the Holy Spirit continues the work of Jesus in the world

Year 5
The gifts of the Holy Spirit and the gifts each child has
Their use in building up the community

Year 6
The Holy Spirit and its place in the Trinity
The Holy Spirit as the power to love

Prayer flowchart

You will notice that in each of the sections of the syllabus there are worship and prayer ideas for each class. As well as involving the children in these worship celebrations, the syllabus allocates to each year its own exercises in prayer development. The tendency in primary schools has been to pray with all the children in very similar ways, irrespective of development. But by following a careful plan you can be sure that the children are being encouraged to pray in different ways. So therefore each year has its own prayer experiences moving from:

Reception and Year 1
Making up their own prayers and praying in a spontaneous fashion
Learning to pray regularly at different points in the day
to help the children to see their prayer life as something totally integrated and natural
Learning the words of the Hail Mary, Our Father, Sign of the Cross

Year 2
Building on the previous year but now learning to spend a little longer each time
The introduction of simple scripture verses to help prayer. Glory be.

Year 3
Building space for silence into the longer times of prayer
Learning to be still, quiet, listening. Prayer in our hearts.

Year 4
Learning to use some traditional methods of prayer
and to adapt them to their needs, for example, the Rosary, litanies

Year 5
Using all the above as well as introducing the children
to images and symbols as a way into prayer

Year 6
The offering of our lives as a prayer
Learning to see how everything that we do can be given to God
Making our lives a prayer

The language used in prayer can sometimes be a barrier. Even prayers as well known and as frequently recited as the Hail Mary and Our Father are pretty meaningless to most infant children, and even to many junior school children. However, this does not mean that they cannot be taught, and the language explained to the children in a meaningful way. In the primary school we are limiting ourselves in the choice of formal traditional prayers to prayers that can be treated in this way. It is our experience that making children recite prayers in a language which is completely foreign and inaccessible does not help their prayer development and contradicts our attempts to make prayer an everyday, many-times-a-day experience.

It is important that many of the beautiful prayers that belong to our Catholic tradition be taught, but it is more appropriate that they be introduced to the children at a more advanced level. This in no way denies the children access, but just saves the richness and the beauty of the language for a time when it can be appreciated. These prayers will be integrated into the secondary school syllabus.

Using the creed as a checklist

This course is based on the Church's year, which ensures that all doctrinal subjects are covered, but you can also use this checklist.

Creation	1T, 2T, 2L, 3T, 4L
Incarnation	1A, 1C, 1Ep, 1Can, 2A, 2C, 4A, 4C, 5S, 6C, 6Can
Trinity	6P
Life and teaching	2A, 2C, 2E, 2Can, 3A, 3P, 4A, 5C, 5E
Discipleship	2C, 2L, 3E, 3Sf, 4Sf, 5W, 5T, 5E, 5L, 5P, 6W, 6A, 6C, 6Ep, 6L, 6E
Redemption and Reconciliation	1E, 1L, 2E, 2S, 3L, 3E, 5E, 6L
Resurrection	2As, 2E, 3P, 4E, 5E, 6As
Judgement	2L, 6As, 6L
Kingdom, Justice	3C, 3E, 3Can, 3L, 4E, 4Can, 4L, 4E, 4S, 5S, 5Can, 5C, 5As, 6C, 6L
Spirit and Church	1P, 2P, 3P, 4P, 5As, 5P, 6P
Sacraments	1W, 1As, 1S, 2As, 2P, 2S, 3L, 3S, 4A, 4C, 4E, 4S, 5As, 5S
Story	1AS, 1W, 2W, 2L, 2P, 2S, 3W, 3As, 3A, 3P, 4T, 4As, 4S, 4P, 5T
Mission and Calling	1Sf, 2P, 2Sf, 3As, 3P, 3Sf, 4W, 4E, 4P, 4Sf, 5T, 5P, 5Sf, 6S

Abbreviations

A	Advent
As	All Souls / All Saints
C	Christmas
Can	Candlemas

E	Easter
Ep	Epiphany
L	Lent
P	Pentecost
S	Saints
Sf	Sending forth
T	Giving thanks
W	Welcome

The numbers indicate the year group.

Assessment and record-keeping

The class teacher has a series of record sheets for each pupil which will be completed during the year. These are based on the lay-out and content of the syllabus but statements have been devised to give a clear and concrete account of what a child should know at the end of each unit, what (s)he should have done (e.g. completed work in book) or taken part in (e.g. a ceremony, discussion, etc.) and what (s)he should have experienced and understood.

The method for assessing each of these should be left to the discretion of the teacher. It should be kept simple and to the point.

The teacher's reasons for filling in the sheet as below

Patricia explained clearly where things belong in the classroom.

She could say what family, school or class she belonged to, as well as to the family of God.

She missed being welcomed during the first week, owing to absence from school (on holiday), but she did take part in the whole-school celebration.

She made clear in conversation that she knew she was important to God, her family and to the teacher but felt she hadn't got any friends in school to play with.

PUPIL RECORD SHEET

Name: Patricia Reynolds
Class: 1

THEME	WHAT PUPIL KNOWS		WHAT PUPIL TOOK PART IN OR HAS DONE		WHAT PUPIL HAS EXPERIENCED OR UNDERSTOOD	
Welcome	what the word 'belong' means	✓	being welcomed	✗	(s)he is important to God	✓
	what (s)he belongs to	✓	a celebration with friends	✓	to family	✓
					to teacher	✓
					to other children	✗
etc...						

To the headteacher

Sharing this information with other staff

Such record sheets will enable you to see at a glance where your pupils are in regard to their part of the syllabus.

It is very important to see that each class teacher takes time to share this information at the end of the year with the teacher taking over the class.

Accurate records will greatly assist the class teacher in writing more accurate and meaningful reports for parents.

Sharing this information with parents

Many headteachers are frequently challenged to demonstrate to parents exactly what is being taught. Claims that pupils are not learning enough doctrine, etc. can be dealt with quickly and easily by showing parents the syllabus and the record sheets.

Sharing this information with governors

Governors are responsible for the whole of the curriculum and often find difficulty in understanding what is actually being taught in RE. It is important to share *The Promise of the Rainbow* with the governors at an early stage and to help them to see what is being taught at each stage.

Part 4

THE BACKGROUND

From pilot to publication: the process and evaluation

With the passing of the Education Reform Act in 1988 many teachers began to be worried that Religious Education was going to be squeezed out by the demands of the new curriculum. Teachers were swamped with new directives and initiatives making new demands on the limited amount of classroom time. From all quarters the warning bells were ringing that teachers just could not cope and needed more help. What was needed was a clearly defined syllabus that showed how time for religious education could be found and how it relates to the rest of the curriculum.

This question about time for religious education and about its infusion in the rest of the curriculum also concerns teachers in the United States and Canada.

The document *Vision and Values* poses many of the same questions for the United States as are being raised in England. *Moment of Promise*, the Canadian challenge from the Ontario Bishops, also raises the same issues regarding the infusion of Christian teaching into the whole curriculum, and this question has been sharpened in Canada by the appearance of the first Catholic schools within the state system.

The Rome document, *The Distinctive Nature of Religious Education in the Catholic School*, and the work of the English and Welsh bishops through the National Project all identify the need for very clear definitions, aims and objectives in the area of religious education within the context of the whole school.

Identifying the issues

All those documents echo the same message — the need to make tangible and real ways of teaching Christian doctrine, the experience of being a worshipping community and the living out of Christian moral values in today's world.

Coming on to the market are many excellent initiatives on both sides of the Atlantic. What we were seeking was a structure which encompassed the whole curriculum of a school and provided at the same time a clearly defined religious education syllabus.

How this was done

Ten schools were initially selected on an ad hoc basis to begin the process of asking themselves the basic question: *what are we here for that is significantly different from what is provided by every other excellent school in the area which does not have a particular Christian affiliation?*

Very quickly our schools realized that they did not have the monopoly on being caring and loving schools. Other schools too had excellent standards, cared about the whole school community, had strong home–school links, and looked outwards to the wider community, so what was it that we were trying to do that justified having a dual system?

Our schools spent some considerable time determining

> (a) what they believed they were doing;
> (b) what parents saw them to be doing;
> (c) what children experienced;
> (d) what the wider community thought they were doing.

Gathering the information

As this information was gathered, schools began to see that for the most part many of their staff could not articulate what was the distinctive nature of a Catholic school beyond saying, 'Well, we're a Catholic school. It's very hard to define. It's in the atmosphere and everything we do, but we can't say what it is.'

Direction and definition

Headteachers very quickly realized that if this answer had been given in any other area of the curriculum it would have been wholly unacceptable. If teachers can't articulate and define what they are doing and how they are doing it and where they hope to go, there is every possibility that they are not doing it at all.

This may seem a hard criticism but we have to be able to define our terms and understand what it is that we are trying to do.

What the teachers realized was that they needed to identify and name exactly what Christian teaching and experiences they wanted their particular pupils to have at every stage of their development. They needed to look at each part of the hidden curriculum as well as the formal curriculum and identify exactly where the Christian teaching was explicit and also where and how it was implicit.

Monitoring

This needed to be monitored in some way. It needed to be recorded; and the ways in which it was being experienced, taught and understood needed to be evaluated. Teachers realized that they were not in the business of measuring faith. What they were keen to establish was a clearly defined method of seeing what is being learnt and where. The whole curriculum had to be taken apart piece by piece and we had to ask the question each time:

'Why are we teaching this?'

'What's the long-term aim?'

'How are we going to do it in a way that shows the relationship between this particular discipline and our Christian faith and lifestyle?'

'What are the children learning which differs from what we think we are teaching?'

Finding a structure

Having defined what we were trying to do (much of this thinking is now encompassed in the document *Safeguarding the Distinctive Nature of Education in a Catholic School*, Westminster Diocese), we looked for a structure for a religious education syllabus. After two years of working on this we realized that our starting-point was wrong. We had been looking at the details of a curriculum which in fact needed to be seen as a whole, and the school's life needed to be seen as a whole. Therefore we had to begin with the leader of the Catholic school community, who carried the responsibility for the whole school, rather than just one aspect.

The headteacher as the starting-point

The headteacher is this leader. If we say headteachers are the leaders of their communities then they have to be seen to be such. The heads of the pilot schools had no problem with identifying their professional role as headteacher of an educating community. But the moment we went into 'How are you different from your neighbour?' we were again on sticky ground. What followed was quite remarkable.

Beginning anew

We started with a large blank sheet of paper stretching over many desks — the whole teaching staff and where possible non-teaching staff, plus parish priest, gathered around the blank paper and we literally started from scratch. We put aside the National Curriculum, we put out of our minds every book we had ever known, and each person said how they saw the head as the leader of the Catholic community. What was the head's own personal witness to Christian values, the witness of his or her prayer life, and the moral values that were inculcated in the daily living of the school?

A realistic model of Church

The group looked at a *realistic model of Church* for their school community, recognizing that there was a possibility that many of their children had little or no experience of parish life. This varied from school to school. Some schools had as high as 80 per cent Mass attendance on a regular basis; others were as low as 15 per cent, but what everybody recognized was that this school community was a very definite expression of Church. Parents, for a whole range of reasons, some expressed and some unexpressed, had opted out or felt excluded from parish life. But what they did feel they could do was send their children to a Catholic school. The groups recognized that parents had placed on them very high expectations, that by sending their children to a Catholic school they hoped to solve the problem of bringing them up as Catholics. It took time for schools to come to terms with what they could reasonably do and what they could not begin to undertake. The school is not the home and it is not the parish, but it can adapt, and many have, to offer our children and the future Church a positive and enriching experience and the exciting challenge of being a Christian in today's world . . .

Headteachers began to see how necessary it was for them to be able to articulate their Christian leadership, and for the whole school to actually see them in this role. *The Promise of the Rainbow* is the fruit of two years' hard work by many headteachers.

Moving on

Our next step was to look at what each teacher, starting with the reception class, felt was most important for their children to experience, be taught and come to understand in the year that they were together. We started always with the Christian teaching and values. We then looked at what the National Curriculum presented for that age group and we looked for the theology that would underpin that teaching. Each teacher wrote up the syllabus in this way. We used the framework of the liturgical cycle of the year because it is the most ancient teaching tradition that we have. We looked carefully for progression and development at each level.

Pacing the pilot

Some schools found that the pace of the pilot work was too much, with the onslaught of the National Curriculum; and so we modified the amount of material that each school was working on. After a year two schools had to drop out for a while because of the loss of staff and the difficulty of bringing new staff on board as well as keeping up with all the national initiatives. A year later both those schools had opted back into the pilot work, but it was important not to overload already overworked and tired teachers.

Making it real: turning theory into practice

As the teachers began to piece together the new RE syllabus each section was piloted and evaluated and subsequently rewritten. Wherever possible much of the good practice that was found in the classrooms was relayed to the pupils' books and teacher's book which are now in preparation. The vast majority of the ideas come directly from the classrooms. My role was simply to have the overview of the whole development, to monitor and compile the findings of each teacher. It was then written up in draft form and sent back for further piloting and criticism.

Links across the Atlantic

As the text began to take shape the Diocese of Colorado, under the direction of Sister Joseph-Marie Kassel, the Schools Superintendent, took up the ideas and began to work alongside Westminster in the pilots. This brought a diversity to the whole project and was mutually enriching. Two of the team travelled to Colorado to introduce the pilot and meet with the schools who had expressed the desire to take part. Links were also forged with Ontario through a visit by two representatives from the diocese who were looking into the dual system of education in Britain, and the ways in which Catholic schools could keep their distinctive nature whilst being part of the State system. This also led to a two-way exchange and the cross-fertilization of ideas between Westminster and Ontario. Interestingly the same needs were being felt in each of the three countries.

Results

Our aim had been to discover a means of delivering the whole school curriculum within a Catholic Christian context. The production of *The Promise of the Rainbow* and *The Rainbow People* was one tangible result. Just as significant was what happened in the different pilot schools. Headteachers noticed a significant improvement in the integration of disciplines within the curriculum. Some teachers had reacted to the National Curriculum and testing by moving into subject-based teaching, rather than topic-based teaching. What the pilot did was not only centralize religious education in the whole curriculum but reaffirm teachers in their ability to use their professional skills in the way that they knew best, making the links, teaching in a style that was child-centred, though teacher-led. The classrooms took on a more integrated and lively appearance, with display work depicting the centrality of the Christian lifestyle. The children began to have a clearer identity, to know why they were in that particular school and to understand that they were members of the Christian community. The whole life experience within the school began to have a consistent message. Teachers stopped taking things for granted, and clearly named and identified what was distinctive and unique.

Level of planning

Because of the need to identify clearly specific Christian teaching, lessons had to be meticulously planned on a half-termly basis. Teachers from across the age-range discussed what they were doing in their class. This led to an increase in awareness amongst teachers of the needs of children at the different age-levels and the need for clear record-keeping for each child. This conversation also led to a clearer and deeper understanding of the need for continuity between the age levels, and eliminated the common pitfall of repeating work that had been done in other years. This had proved to be an area which needed some considerable attention in religious education. For example, Christmas tended to be taught and experienced in much the same way throughout the whole school. Infant children tended to be given a watered-down and potted version of what middle and top juniors were doing. Teachers became aware of the need to ask 'What is the Church teaching at this time of the year which is appropriate to the age group I am teaching?'

Record-keeping

The need to keep clear records became essential. In this way it was possible for the teachers to see at any given moment exactly what the children had taken part in, what they had been taught and what they had understood. Much discussion ensued throughout the whole pilot exercise about assessing religious education, and these three roots, of teaching, worship and values, became our guidelines.

Links with the parents

Parents often asked what was going on. The pilot highlighted ways in which the school could give parents a clear outline of exactly what was being taught, and ways in which they could be involved more fully in their children's religious education.

Links with the clergy

A clearer understanding between the school and the clergy proved to be one of the most helpful developments of this pilot exercise. Schools realized again how essential it was to keep the clergy involved in what they were trying to do. Many clergy too told us that this was a more valuable opportunity for keeping in touch and being present to children than they had ever known. As a result we added a parish section on all celebration planning sheets.